FATIMA

APOCALYPSE

NOW

by Fr. Paul Trinchard, S.T.L.

MAETA
METAIRIE LOUISIANA

Published by MAETA

Printed in the United States of America

ISBN 1-889168-09-2

Library of Congress Catalog Card Number
2001126813

MAETA
PO BOX 6012
METAIRIE LA 70009-6012

Apocalyptic Vision of St. John Bosco

In the midst of this endless sea, two solid columns, a short distance apart, soar high into the sky. One is surmounted by a statue of the Immaculate Virgin, at whose feet a large inscription reads: 'Auxilium Christianorum' [Help of Christians or Holy Mary]. The other, far loftier and sturdier, supports a Host of proportionate size, and bears beneath it the inscription: 'Salus credentium' ['Salvation of believers' in Holy Mass].

The flagship commander–the Roman Pontiff [the martyred Marian Pope]–standing at the helm, strains every muscle to steer his ship between the two columns, from whose summit hang many anchors, and strong hooks linked to chains. The entire enemy fleet closes in to intercept and sink the flagship at all costs. They bombard it with everything they have: books and pamphlets, incendiary bombs, firearms, cannons...Beaked prows ram the flagship again and again, but to no avail, as, unscathed and undaunted, it keeps on its course.

Meanwhile, enemy cannons blow up; firearms and beaks fall to pieces; ships crack up and sink to the bottom. In blind fury, the enemy takes to hand-to-hand combat, cursing and blaspheming. Suddenly the Pope falls, seriously

FATIMA
APOCALYPSE
NOW

Fr. Paul Trinchard, S.T.L.

wounded. He is instantly helped up, but, struck a second time, dies. A shout of victory rises up from the enemy...But no sooner is the pope dead than another takes his place...the new Pope [the glorious Marian Pope] guides the ship right up to the two columns and comes to rest between them; he makes it fast with a light chain that hangs from the bow to an anchor of the column on which stands the Host; and with another light chain which hangs from the stern, he fastens it at the opposite end to another anchor hanging from the column on which stands the Immaculate Virgin.

May 30, 1862

"You shall be as gods knowing (gnostically deciding) good and evil" (Ge 3:5).

The Woman Clothed With the Sun

Dedicated to the Immaculate Heart of Mary and the Sacred Heart of Jesus.

When Our Lady first appeared at Fatima, the villagers asked the children what they saw. They reported seeing *"a woman clothed with the sun"* (Apoc 12:1). Does this not "sign" the Apocalyptic confrontation (as foretold in Genesis)? If so, the Fatima apocalypse is now.

The Third Secret promises that Holy Mary will be victorious. Holy Church will materialize: *"In the end, my Immaculate Heart will triumph."* This sign of Our Lady of the Apocalypse clothed with the sun teaches that Holy Mary comes to us through a properly functioning sun (Holy Church). Somehow, mystically speaking, Holy Mary brings us Holy Church and vice-versa.

Fatima's subsequent sign of the aberrant sun was a portent of the dysfunctional/malicious New Order existential church. The Fatima Message (and the vision of St. John Bosco) disclose that such a Church has hope only in the Marian Pope and his activating the Fatima opportunity/command.

Table of Contents

About the Author

Fr. Paul Trinchard was ordained as a Jesuit (6/7/66) and is now a retired diocesan priest. He has a Master degree in physics and has studied the philosophy of science at Columbia University, San Francisco State, American University and Hebrew University. He earned a Master degree in philosophy. He also earned a pontifical Licentiate in Sacred Theology, specializing in Paul Tillich. Fr. Trinchard is an internationally acclaimed authority on the Mass and on Fatima.

Other works by Fr. Trinchard are:

All About Salvation
New Age New Mass
New Mass In Light of the Old
Holy Mary Holy Mass
Russia's Error
Pray the Holy Mass
My Basic Missal
The Abbot & Me On Liturgy
The Awesome Fatima Consecrations
Apostasy Within
God's Word
The Mass That Made Padre Pio

INTRODUCTION

Fatima Apocalypse Now

Fatima Apocalypse Now spells out the awesome meaning and significance of the Fatima Message. Also, on the negative or "cleansing" side, Fatima's Message discloses Rome's gray or black propaganda concerning Fatima and its "Third Secret."

In these apocalyptic times, Mary's Remnant (described in Apoc 12) will be saved. Such as these realize and live being saved by "the Blood of the Lamb," the Canonized Mass. This book is dedicated to the Sacred Heart of Jesus and the Immaculate Heart of Mary; and to MAETA (Marian End Times Apostolate). May devotion to Christ, His Mother, the Roman Catholic Church and the Fatima Message (as explained in this book) hasten the times of the Fatima Blessings, when the existential

11

church and Russia will be converted; devotion to the Sacred Heart of Jesus and the Immaculate Heart of Mary will flourish; ecclesial and social peace will be manifested; and, most importantly for us sinners, many souls will be saved from eternal Hell. Our Lady of Fatima, pray for us!

CHAPTER 1

KEY FATIMA YEARS

**My God, I believe, I adore, I hope, I love Thee!
I ask pardon for those who do not believe, do
not adore, do not hope in and do not love Thee.**
Prayer given by the Angel of Peace, Fatima, 1916

Ultimately and essentially, *peace* is freedom from sin and sin's effect–Hell. Without such freedom, there is no peace. The Holy Mass, the Holy Sacrifice of Christ, is the source, sustenance and summit of any and all peace.

What message of peace did the Angel of Peace bring? The angels announced the Saviour to the world two thousand years ago. Fatima's most timely angelic message proclaims that the Saviour of the Elect comes to this earth within each Holy Mass. From its inception, Fatima focuses on Holy Mass.

However, to receive the salutary message fruitfully, one must first be led to a firm belief in Reality–in God as He is; and, in man as a sinner; and *not God and man as sinners imagine them to be.* A strong, salutary belief in *God as He is* and *one's self as a sinner* will produce an overwhelming personal conviction of one's infinitely important problem and task: to come to the knowledge of, belief in and conformity to (the salutary solution) Jesus Christ and His Salutary Will (thus, to sanctify and to save one's own soul).

In the spring of 1916, God initiated the awesome apocalyptic Fatima Message. The Angel of Fatima introduced himself: "I am the Angel [messenger] of Peace." Next, the children (representing Mary's Remnant) are led to realize that pardon for sin can come only through or from the Mass: Christ's Holy Sacrifice, the Canonized Mass (as dogmatically defined by the Council of Trent). In sign, symbol and reality, the children, reflecting man's salutary progression, were brought by God into the Holy Mass. Lucia narrates what happened to the children at the Angel's visit in the fall of 1916.

> **As soon as we arived at the Loca do Cabeco, we knelt down, with our foreheads touching the ground, and began to repeat the prayer of the Angel: 'My God, I believe, I adore, I hope, and I love Thee...'**

I don't know how many times we had repeated this prayer, when an extraordinary light shone upon us. We sprang up to see what was happening, and beheld the Angel. The Angel was holding a chalice in his left hand, with the Host suspended above it, from which some drops of blood fell into the chalice. Leaving the chalice suspended in the air, the angel knelt down beside us and made us repeat three times:

'Most Holy Trinity, Father, Son and Holy Ghost, I adore Thee profoundly, and I offer Thee the most precious Body, Blood, Soul and Divinity of Our Lord and Saviour, Jesus Christ, present in all the tabernacles throughout the world, in reparation for all the outrages, sacrileges and indifferences with which He Himself is offended. And through the infinite merits of His most Sacred Heart and the Immaculate Heart of Mary, I beg of Thee the conversion of poor sinners.' [Here is the only Source of conversion and salvation–the Holy Mass, which produces the Holy Sacrament.]

Then, rising, he took the chalice and the Host in his hands. He gave the Sacred Host to me, and shared the Blood from the chalice between Jacinta and Francisco, saying as he did so: 'Take and drink the Body and Blood of Jesus Christ, horribly outraged by ungrateful men! Make reparation for their crimes and console your God.'

Once again, he prostrated on the ground and

**repeated with us, three times more, the same
prayer: 'Most Holy Trinity...' and then
disappeared.'**
Lucia's account, *The Whole Truth About Fatima*

Note the pattern. The children's confession of personal
sinfulness, plus their belief in, adoration of, hope in and
love of God, as it were, attracted God to bring them His
Greatest Gift: Holy Sacrament, the Fruit of Holy
Sacrifice; most likely, the Fruit of the Canonized Mass
celebrated by St. Padre Pio.

Holy Sacrament is the abiding Fruit of Holy Mass. Also,
Holy Sacrament is the Fruit of Holy Mary. Therefore,
quite logically, the next year, Our Lady appeared.
Looking very sad, Our Lady said:

> **Pray. Pray very much, and make sacrifice for
> sinners; for many souls go to hell, because there
> are none to sacrifice themselves and to pray for
> them.**
> Our Lady of Fatima

Fatima Essentials

Vain (both proud and unrealistic or useless) thinking
leads many to conclude that the attainment of Heaven, of
union with Jesus and Mary is "so simple as to be

automatic." Fatima brings one back to Reality. Generally speaking, Original Sin, compounded by Actual Sin, makes personal salvation "very, very difficult to attain." As Blessed Jacinta stated: "Many many, souls go to Hell." Therefore, souls must be prayed and sacrificed into Heaven and out of going to Hell. Again and again, the Fatima children prayed and sacrificed for sinners–for sinners to be saved from eternal Hell.

The Fatima Revelations

With these Fatima essentials in mind, one can better appreciate the "three revelations of Fatima." The First Revelation addressed the primary, solitary and infinitely important need for each individual to be saved from Hell. The Second Revelation emphasized not only the social matrix of sin; but also, social or national punishments as being the effects of sins. Lastly, the first and last sentences of the Third Revelation were presented at Fatima on October 13, 1917.

For many decades, the main body of the Third Revelation was turned into a secret by wicked clergymen. Then, in 2000, Pope/Rome issued an *alleged* Third Revelation accompanied by a wicked exegesis.

In 1917, on a day they would never forget, their loving Mother showed these children a horribly frightening vision of Hell. Men and angels writhed in indescribably painful agony, which will never end. After this vision, Mother Mary gave us God's special antidote for man's "normal fate." Devotion to Holy Mary (which devotion would lead to Holy Mass) was God's apocalyptic gift to modern man.

> **You have seen Hell where the souls of poor sinners go. To save them, God wishes to establish in the world, devotion to my Immaculate Heart.** [Here is the First Revelation of Fatima.]

> [Fatima's Second Revelation now follows.] **If what I am going to tell you is done, many souls will be saved and there will be peace. The war is going to end. But if men do not cease offending God, another and worse war will begin under the reign of Pius XI. When you see a night illumined by a strange light, know that this is the sign God gives you that He is going to punish the world for its crimes, by means of war, famine and persecutions against the Church and the Holy Father.**

> **To prevent this, I shall come to ask for the consecration of Russia to my Immaculate Heart and reparatory Communion on the first five Saturdays of every month.**

If my requests are heeded, Russia will be converted and there will be peace. If not, Russia will spread her errors throughout the world, stirring up wars and persecutions against the Church. The good will be martyred, the Holy Father will have much to suffer, various nations will be annihilated. [Next, the first sentence of the Third Revelation of Fatima is disclosed.] **In Portugal, the dogma of the faith will always be retained, etc.**

At this point, there would normally be revealed the third part of the message, the "Third Secret," which (one can contend) is the announcement of the great apostasy of the Church in her head and members, following the conciliar reform–an apostasy that deepens daily, calling forth God's increased wrath–until the awesome day of papal and episcopal consecration of Russia and vowed ecclesial rePARation. This Fatima revelation informs us of the happy conclusion to the Third Revelation:

In the end, my Immaculate Heart will triumph. The Holy Father will consecrate Russia to me and a time of peace will be given to the world.

[This last disclosed sentence of the Third Revelation of Fatima, along with the previously cited first sentence, are noticeably absent from Rome's Millennial Fatima Message.]

Remember the number of the Apocalyptic BEASTS–"666." This represents the New World Order. The New World Order is man replacing God or man worshiped in the place of God. The Second and Third Revelations of Fatima assure us that unless we repent and unless the Church renounces the New World Novus Ordo and vows (both liturgical and fiducial) rePARation:

Russia's (the First Beast's) **ERRORS will spread throughout the world; and, the apostate existential church body's** (the Second Beast's) **ERRORS will lead many to lose the Faith and be damned into eternal Hell.**

Political leaders, legislators, and judges increasingly presume and mandate a "man-centered," Godless or faithless society. Russia's (the First Beast's) errors are becoming our "truth." Russia's errors are spreading throughout the world, especially, within the U.S.A.

Liturgically, (as well as, in the practice of religion) throughout most of the world, the New Order (Novus Ordo) liturgy and religion have sacrilegiously replaced the Christ-given faith and morals of Apostolic Tradition. All "man-exalting and God-dethroning" liturgies and religions constitute the Second Beast (Apoc 13.).

In the fall of 1917, the Communist Revolutionists conquered Russia. In that same year, God's end-times (or apocalyptic) clock began to tick when the Balfour Declaration established Jewish occupancy of Palestine.

In 1929, the Salutary Theophany of the Canonized Mass (to Sr. Lucy in her convent chapel at Tuy, Spain) climaxed the Fatima Message. (This theophany will be treated in detail later.) For now, note that this vision "solidified" the intimate union of devotion to Holy Mary and devotion to Holy Mass. Holy Mary and Holy Mass define or characterize Holy Church–the one and only God-given means of salvation from Hell.

It is interesting to note that, immediately after the Holy Mass Theophany of Tuy, Our Lady told humanity that the time had come for Russia to be consecrated to her Immaculate Heart (as foretold in the Second Revelation). Why? Urgency was increasing: Holy Mary and Holy Mass would soon be sacrileged. In the words of La Salette, *"Rome would become the seat of antichrist."* Only the Holy Father, the Marian Pope, can bring about Holy Mary, Holy Mass and Holy Church through his God-given power to "create" Holy Russia.

In 1929, the Russian Communist government took over the weakened Russian Orthodox (Schismatic) Church. In that same year, God's message at Tuy disclosed that the conversion of Russia, along with the enjoyment of world peace, could be obtained only by the Pope and his subservient bishops abandoning the political means of humanistic geopolitical designs in favor of embracing and implementing God's Fatima-provided faith-dependent methodology.

Hopefully, the twenty-first century will witness this awesome apocalyptic day of Fatima Consecration. To bring this about, two Marian Popes will materialize.[1] One will be martyred. The other will consecrate Russia as Our Lady demanded: exercising his supreme power over his subservient bishops by ordering them to consecrate Russia with him to the Immaculate Heart of Mary; and, along with him to "vow reparation." It is of utmost ecclesial importance that this Marian Pope (along with his subservient bishops) *implement fiducial and liturgical reparation, re-establish what was always 'par.'* " Fatima and the ecclesial Church depend on it.

Thus, Liturgical reparation will restore the Canonized Mass as the one and only Mass of the Catholic Church. Russia, being consecrated by the Pope, will become Holy Russia. An era of peace will come to the whole world. Of infinite and eternal importance, many (instead of very

---

[1]

Why two Marian Popes? From the prophetic visions of St. John Bosco, from what we already know about the Third Secret, Jacinta's seeing a pope being persecuted and "attacked;" and, Rome's alleged Millennial "Third Secret," one is led to conjecture and presume that there will be two Marian Popes: one will be martyred and the other will bring the Church into the era of Fatima Blessing.

few) souls will be brought into eternal beatific bliss.

At this point, one is led to seek historical perspective. In general, the modern pre-1929 popes (relying on their "graced natures and papal charisma") did what they could, only to become aware of their inability. They turned to God for help. The Fatima Message was the answer to their prayers.

On the other hand, post-1929, and, especially, post-1960 popes, having lost or rejected "faith in the Fatima Message" pursued a course of geopolitical strivings to bring a New Order type of peace to mankind. God has damned to failure this secular humanist course of action.

God will grant peace and spiritual prosperity only through His Marian Pope. When enough are sufficiently praying and sacrificing for God's Fatima-expressed Will to be done, then He will give us the Marian Popes–the Popes who, (believing in and being totally committed to Holy Mary, Holy Mass and the Fatima Message) will bring us out of ever-increasing apocalyptic horrors into an awesome era of Fatima Blessings.

CHAPTER 2

PROPHECY

Prophecy, in the biblical sense, does not mean to predict the future, but to explain the will of God for the present, and, therefore, show the right path to take for the future. A person who foretells what is going to happen responds to the curiosity of the mind, which wants to draw back the veil on the future. The prophet speaks to the blindness of will and of reason, and declares the will of God...The prophetic word is a warning or a consolation, or both together....
Carefully selected passages from Cardinal Ratzinger on Rome's Millennial Fatima Message, June 26, 2000

At critical times in human history, God intervenes through prophecy by reminding us of the necessity of obeying Him and the resultant blessings which come from conforming to His Revealed Word. Our ecstatic (grace-activated) minds and hearts embrace God's basic (classical and time-critical) revelations. How are God's prophetic and time-critical revelations (both biblical and non-biblical) confirmed? How can one differentiate what is authentically God's Word from man's self-serving fabrications and contrivances of "God's Word?"

The Holy Bible gives the answer. Always, the alleged prophet speaks; short term predictions are made; and these short term predictions are confirmed. Such a confirmation, in itself, establishes the fact that the prophet speaks in the name of God or by the devil's power. Satan's or God's supernatural power must be present, since only such an intelligence can reasonably project (or provide, as in God's providence) certain kinds of "specific predictions" (cf. Mt 24:23-24).

However, when the prophet speaks so as to confirm and "illustrate," or properly apply God's basic revelations; or, so as to bring men to repentance and sanctification, then "the finger of God" is present: God has originated the prophetic message. Being a "good," historically validated, prophetic message, it must originate from God, not from the devil or from human ingenuity. Therefore, one can trust its message, long-term predictions or subsequent fulfillment. Lastly, true prophecy brings one to God, not to the prophet. God never prophesies through an individual to exalt that individual.

CHAPTER 3

FATIMA: GOD-GIVEN PROPHECY

The Fatima Prophecy was proven to be authentic because its short-term prophecies were subsequently fulfilled (e.g. the prediction of a spectacular miracle on October 13, 1917). It is thus an undeniable fact that the Fatima Message comes from God.

The Fatima Message is not the pious creation of Sister Lucy, as the theory of Fr. Dhanis (the papal advisor on Fatima since Pope Pius XII) contends. At this point, one must emphasize the danger of underestimating the sacrilegious effect of Pope/Rome's bias against the Fatima Message. This is illustrated by the following incident. Immediately after the June 26, 2000 distortion of Fatima and its Third Secret by Rome, a local television program addressed Rome's Millennial Fatima Message. Typically, (in the spirit of Fr. Dhanis) an articulate archbishop reduced the Fatima Message to gnostic triviality and irrelevance.

Then, an unusual or atypical nun brought us back to reality. She noted that, in spite of the establishment's party line to debunk, trivialize and sacrilege the Fatima Message, the fact remains that, on October 13, 1917, [thirty-three years to the day after Pope Leo XIII's apocalyptic vision, which led him to compose the "Leonine Prayers" to be said after Mass] the children of Fatima, as well as the crowds of people present at Fatima, saw (an inter-subjectively verifiable) vision–or spectacle–at the Cova da Iria.

On this day, at noon, 70,000 people (from devout Catholics to dedicated Masons) saw the miracle of the sun. That miracle authenticated the Message of Fatima beyond all doubt. Not even the Old Testament prophets could claim a more impressive prophetic credential from God. This validating miracle was reported even in the liberal, anti-clerical, Masonic newspaper, *O Seculo*. The newspaper reported:

> **We saw the huge crowd turn toward the sun, which appeared at its zenith, clear of the clouds. It resembled a flat plate of silver, and it was possible to stare at it without the least discomfort. It did not burn the eyes. We would say that it produced an eclipse. Then a tremendous cry rang out and the crowd nearest us were heard to shout:'Miracle!...Miracle!... Marvel!...Marvel!...'**

Before the dazed eyes of the people, whose attitude transported us to biblical times, and who, dumbfounded, heads uncovered, contemplated the blue of the sky, the sun trembled, it made strange and abrupt movements, outside of all cosmic laws, 'the sun danced,' according to the typical expression of the peasants.
Fatima Crusader, Summer 2000, p. 16, quoting the newspaper, *O Seculo,* Oct. 15, 1917

Other Fatima predictions were made in 1917 and were fulfilled later on. These, too, confirm that the Fatima Message originated from God.

Under the reign of Pius XI, another and worse war will begin.
Our Lady of Fatima, 1917

How sad it is to see our Mother announce what she knows is bound to happen in the near future. For us, it is in the past. But the prophecy is dated with an accuracy far superior to that of the historians' works. It was indeed in 1938 *under the reign of Pius XI,* whose role and existence no one on earth could have foreseen in 1917 (especially, the three little shepherds of Aljustrel) that World War II was begun.[1]

---

[1]

See *The Whole Truth About Fatima,* Frere Michel, Volume 2, pp. 660-670 for proof of this statement. To order: 1-800-263-8160.

When you see a night illumined by a strange light, know that this is the sign God is giving you that He is about to punish the world for its crimes.

Our Lady of Fatima, 1917

In the year 1917, Our Lady gave the sign and the date of the beginning of the chastisement. The sign, which was a night illumined by a strange light (the 25th of January, 1938), inspired Hitler to start World War II. On the following 13th of March, German troops invaded Austria. Hitler was thus beginning his conquest of Europe (which was initially backed by Stalin).

For Sr. Lucy, the seer of Fatima, it was the beginning of the *"horrible, horrible"* war, which God had decreed *to punish the world for its crimes.*[1] In August, 1931, Our Lord predicted such papal disobedience to Fatima's command:

They did not wish to heed My demand. Like the King of France, they will repent and do it, but it will be late.

on-going Fatima prophecy, Aug.,1931, Our Lord to Sr. Lucy

---

[1]

This prediction has been confirmed by "disobedience to" and "rejection of" the Fatima Message by post-Fatima popes, climaxing in the sacrilegious Pope/Rome Millennial Fatima Message issued in 2000.

CHAPTER 4

DISCOVERING THE THIRD REVELATION

The question arises: Is the Pope/Rome millennial disclosure and exegesis of the Fatima Message credible? How can one verify the truth of the Millennial Fatima Message as presented by Pope/Rome 2000?

One can easily disprove the credibility/authenticity of Rome's Millennial Fatima Message by comparing it with what is already known to be the specific contents of the Third Revelation of Fatima; other Fatima revelations; and the generic tone of Fatima and other God-given "prophecies" or holy writings. Thus, one can perceive that the inductive process is based upon God-given compatible and past, Church approved revelations.

Because Cardinal Ratzinger was one of the few who actually read the Third Revelation of Fatima, he provides a sound direction for the use of inductive reasoning to come to an understanding of the contents of the Third Revelation of Fatima. In *The Ratzinger Report,* he told us where to look, as well as, how to look.

> On August 15, 1984, noted Italian journalist Vittorio Messori interviewed Cardinal Ratzinger. The interview became the book noted above.
>
> "Have you read the so-called Third Secret?"
>
> The reply is immediate and dry: "Yes, I have read it."
>
> After further probing questions, the Cardinal said: "The Holy Father deems that it would add nothing to what a Christian must know from Revelation and also from the Marian apparitions approved by the Church in their known contents..."
>
> *The Ratzinger Report,* p. 109

In Accord With Other Marian Apparitions

The Third Revelation of Fatima (as Ratzinger himself states in *The Ratzinger Report)* must be in accord with other "Marian apparitions approved by the Church." The inductive argumentation (to discover the generic contents of the Third Revelation) is based upon these other apparitions; as well as, on saintly and papal statements and predictions (which are suggested by, or seem to be in conformity to, or, further elucidate the apocalyptic Fatima Message) as already widely known.

In The Bible

Sister Lucy has assured us that, at least "in effect," we are in the end times. Sister Lucy, when questioned on the contents of the Third Secret, refers us to the Apocalypse.

> **It's in the Gospel and the Apocalypse. Read them.**
> Sister Lucy, *The Whole Truth About Fatima,* Frere Michel de la Saint Trinite, p. 788

Relevant to what is known from the First and Second Revelations (and other statements by Sister Lucy and by reliable Fatima experts, etc.) one can illustrate how the Apocalypse (Chapter 13:11-18) pertains to the Fatima Message and, especially, to the Third Revelation.

Having been cast down upon the earth, Satan is bringing forth the First and Second Beasts of the Apocalypse. The New Age and the New Order come from Satan. Increasingly, this world, which lies in Satan's lap (1 Jo 5:19), will be under the Social and Religious Beast:

> **I saw a Second Beast rise out of the earth. It had two 'horns' like a lamb, but it spoke like a dragon. It exercises authority with the First Beast and makes the earth and its people to worship the First Beast. It works great signs, even making fire come down from heaven...It deceives those who dwell on earth...It slew those who would not worship the image of the Beast...the number of the Beast is the number of Man.**
>
> **Apoc 13:11-18, my version)**

The First Beast is the rule or government of Man by Man according to Man's "God-less" standards. The Second Beast is the "soul" of the First Beast.

The Second Beast is like a lamb. It resembles God's true Church, within which dwells the Lamb of God. Yet, it has the "soul" or spirit of Satan, the dragon.

34

Up to this point, it can be proposed that the Third Revelation of Fatima, according to the Bible, must (at least, generically) concern end-times conditions; or, at least, conditions like unto the end-times. Indeed, do not "false christs" prevail in our day as predicted by Jesus? A "false christ" is a vain (proud and useless) way to be saved, a vain savior.(cf. Mt 24:23-24)

Two Ratzingers

Notice, also, that one can follow the Ratzinger of *The Ratzinger Report* but must reject the Ratzinger of Rome's Millennial Fatima Message. The latter Ratzinger presumes and applies the anti-Fatima Dhanis theories and concludes to the officially approved "party line."[1] Simply stated, the "party line" assures us that any interpretation of the Fatima Message which embarrasses or vilifies Pope/Rome (even of the past) must be rejected and condemned.

Throughout these considerations, each is confronted with

---

[1] Simply stated, Fr. Dhanis reduces the Fatima Message to a vague call to be good. He rejects any and all "embarrassing particulars" as being reducable, in effect, to pious chatter or pietistic and cryptic mystical utterances.

an ultimate test: Will one conform his thinking to God's Message and to Reality–or–to the presently dysfunctional "living magisterium?" Will one opt for Our Lady's Fatima Message or for Rome's Millennial Fatima Message?

Furthermore, the clarity of this choice is often obscured by the employment of an ecclesially popular neo-Hegelian methodology. For example, Ratzinger/Rome's Third Revelation "contradicts itself." Thus, even one who follows Rome is left to choose which "contradictory neo-Hegelian thesis" he will support.

For example, one must choose between the "Sodano affirming Pope" and the "Sodano opposing Pope." On May 13, 2000, Cardinal Sodano disclosed the alleged heart of Rome's Millennial Fatima Message, the alleged "Third Secret" and his official exegesis in the presence of Pope John Paul II.

By way of contrast, however, according to a "Blue Army speaker," the "anti-Sodano" Pope "banged on his prie-dieu" during Sodano's talk. (*Fatima Crusader,*Summer 2000, Pope John Paul II on May 13, 2000 at Fatima) On this same day, (May 13, 2000) Pope John Paul II gave a sermon, which clearly opposed the tone or "spirit" of Sodano's message. In general, the Pope emphasized the apocalyptic nature and extreme relevance of the Fatima Message. In effect, he confirmed "Fatima apocalypse now."

The Pope assured us that we are indeed living now during the fulfillment of biblical prophecy (specifically, the Apocalypse). The Pope confirmed the continued relevance of the Fatima Message when he emphasized that the Bible was written 1900 years ago by command of God to be a guide for our generation in these confusing and very evil times (which are not "past and to be forgotten," as Sodano contended an hour or so later). The Pope assured us of a "live" Fatima message as he warned us that we must be on our guard against the devil (thereby, inferring that we are *not* in an era of Fatima Blessings). (*Fatima Crusader,* Summer 2000, Pope John Paul II on May 13, 2000 at Fatima)

This is a remarkable papal confession, a confession which, in neo-Hegelian dialectic fashion, negates Rome's Millennial (papally approved?) "Fatima Message." In effect, in opposition to the spirit of "Sodano's and (Congregation for the Doctrine of the Faith) Ratzinger's Fatima Message," the Pope assures us that the "Third Secret" is apocalyptic *now.*

Indeed, the Fatima Message refers to the end-times. It refers to apostasy within and to the urgent necessity to be a MAETA–a Marian End Times Apostle.

Other tools of discernment exist–such as attending to what "Fatima experts" (especially, Sister Lucy and the popes), other Church authorities, and previous saints have disclosed relative to these end-times. For example, one knows that the Third Revelation addresses two subjects: the Pope and the Faith.

We learn this from the representative of Pope Pius XII, Father Schweigl, who interrogated Sister Lucy (September 1952) for some time regarding the Third Revelation. He assured us that the "Third Secret concerned two things: the Pope and the loss of Faith" (cf. *Fatima Crusader*, Summer 2000, p. 81).

A Logically Patterned and Developed Message

The First Revelation concerns *individual* moral entities. The Second Revelation concerns *societal* moral entities. Therefore, the Third Revelation must concern the remaining moral entity, the *church*.

The First Revelation assures us that God's wrath comes upon evil individuals. The Second Revelation assures us that God's wrath comes upon evil societies (largely because of the Pope's failure to activate or obey the Fatima command).

To preserve the logical pattern, one is led to conclude that the Third Revelation *must assure* us that God's wrath comes upon the evil existential church. Does it not begin by addressing faithlessness and, thus, an evil church body?

In Portugal, the dogmas of the [Catholic] faith will be preserved.

Obviously, it should continue:

However, elsewhere, the dogmas of faith will be lost and, thus, evil churches flourish.

The First and Second Revelations provide relief from God's wrath:

Be one of Mary's Remnant and be saved from ell. Pray the Marian Pope into existence and save many from Hell.
First Revelation (paraphrased)

The logical pattern continues:

Pray the Marian Pope into existence and then the church will be rePARed. Russia will become Holy Russia and social peace will prevail.
Second Revelation (paraphrased)

To preserve a logical pattern, the Third Revelation (which concludes with the prediction of the glorious Marian Pope) must urge us to pray the Marian Pope into existence. As a consequence, the Church will once again be Holy Church.

Finally, Holy Mary and Holy Mass will once again have their proper, God-given salutary role and purpose within the lives of Catholics. Our Lady (together with popes and saints) has led us to conclude that the Third Revelation of Fatima is awesome; apocalyptic; and urgently applies to our times. Fatima's Apocalyptic Message must concern: a wicked Church; fiducial apostasy within this Church; liturgical apostasy within this Church; God's subsequent wrath and a martyred Pope; the glorious Marian Pope and an era of Fatima Blessings.

CHAPTER 5

FATIMA'S APOCALYPTIC MESSAGE MUST CONCERN AN APOSTATE OR HERETICAL CHURCH

The Church of St. Peter in ruins...many excommunicated clergy, unconcerned and even unaware of their being excommunicated [since, as she correctly observed, they "embraced opinions to which an anathema had been attached"]...the Catholic religion fell into complete decadence as everything pertaining to Protestantism gained the upper hand.
Blessed Anna Emmerich, stigmatist and visionary of nineteenth century

It would seem that Blessed Anna Emmerich had written this in Chicago, yesterday, instead of in Germany in

1820. In 1634, Mother Mary Torres, in Quito, Ecuador, saw that for a large part of the twentieth century *"various heresies will flourish on this earth."*[1]

Today's church is the very worst in the history of Catholicism. Fatima's awesome apocalyptic Message must address this wicked (existential) church, within which we live.

The Revelation *of and to* this wicked church can be broken down further. Fiducial and liturgical apostasy define its wickedness. God's wrath is a consequence of such wickedness. Finally, as in all God-given prophecies to mankind, there is given a solution. The solution is the coming into being of the Marian Popes through our prayers and sacrifices.

There is an outstanding Fatima-related validation of this Fatima contention: the Miracle of the Sun on October 13, 1917. Furthermore, it will be shown throughout this book that the Third Revelation concerns the modern apostate existential church; and, that the Third Revelation was given to impress upon us the urgency to "pray and sacrifice" the Marian Popes into existence.

---

[1]

Heresy is the obstinate post-baptismal denial or doubt of some truth which must be believed with Catholic or Divine Faith *(Revised Code of Canon Law,* No. 751)

The Miracle of the Sun

We say, in truth, that the pit of the abyss is open, from whence St. John saw smoke arise up that darkened the sun...We are horrified, venerable brethren, at seeing with what doctrines, or better said, with what monstrosity of error we find ourselves buried.
Pope Gregory XVI, 1834

Even in 1834, Pope Gregory XVI (who promoted the dogma of the Immaculate Conception) perceived that the church (represented by the sun) would be inundated by error. In 1917, as it were, Fatima would confirm that this "sun analogy" applied to the present ecclesially dysfunctional times:

A. M. Martins, a native of Portugal, presents his reaction to the Miracle of the Sun: What I am able to affirm is that at the exact moment when the wee girl said, 'Look at the Sun. There is the sign that Our Lady spoke of,' all of us saw the sun oscillating and taking on shapes never seen before...Indeed, for six months the children had been saying that there would be a sign, that would make everyone believe in the truth of the apparition of the Lady.
A.M. Martins, *Fatima Caminho da Paz* Fatima, Way of Peace, Augustine Pub. Co., Devon,MCMLXXXIX, pp. 60-63

The "sign" validating Fatima is the aberrant or

malicious, dysfunctional sun, the aberrant or malicious, dysfunctional church, which Fatima foreshadowed and which has characterized these "apocalyptic ecclesial times."

On October 13, 1917, in Fatima, everyone saw the sun–representing the existential church–being not only totally dysfunctional, but also a grave menace to mankind. Previously, on September 13, 1917, many onlookers saw *the cross leaving the sun.* Did this not signify that Christ's Sacrifice would leave the existential church?

> **People should say the rosary every day in order to be fortified against these times of diabolical disorientation, so that we would not allow ourselves to be deceived by false doctrines...A diabolical disorientation is invading the world, deceiving souls! It must be resisted!**
> **Sr. Lucy, Letter to a friend who promoted Marian devotion, from *Letters, 1969-70***
>
> **It is painful to see such great confusion, and in so many persons who occupy positions of responsibility!**
> **Sr. Lucy, Letter to a religious friend, *Letters. 1969-70***

The sun represents the existential church. On October 13, 1917, the sun became aberrant and dysfunctional. It left its appointed orbit. The (post-Vatican II) church, like the sun, became aberrant and dysfunctional. It, too, left its appointed orbit. It degenerated into a human, political organization, which pleases men, not God. Also, like the Fatima sun, it has been eclipsed.

The sun will be darkened and the moon will not shed her light and the stars will fall from heaven.
Prophecy of St. John

The stars, bishops, have fallen. Dysfunctional/malicious bishops have produced the Bishops' Revolt. (The Novus Ordo Church, "invented" by malicious experts, was imposed by bishops under popes who acted as bishops, not popes.) It has become obvious that the aberrant behavior of the sun signifies the eclipse of Holy Church, coloring the establishment church as less divine and more human. Today, each "cafeteria-style Catholic" can be pleased with his own color of heresy. The existential church offers no outspoken, nor effective, opposition.

One must admit...heresies have been propagated in the areas of dogma and morals creating doubt, confusion and rebellion. Even the liturgy has plunged into intellectual and moral relativism and even as far as permissiveness, where everything is allowed.
Pope John Paul II, *L'Osservatore Romano*, Feb. 8, 1981

Believe the Pope. Here, he speaks the truth. Apostasy flourishes within the existential church. Post Vatican Two popes admit this "in their weaker moments."

On June 26, 2000, Pope/Rome intensified and (in a certain sense) "finalized" the Fatima Curse upon its New Order constitution when it issued its Millennial Fatima Message. In the issuance of this "message," Pope/Rome has tried to bury forever, what, for the Vatican, must be an embarrassing and condemnatory Fatima Message. This burial and sacrileging of the Fatima Message was evident even to the Los Angeles Times:

> **The Vatican's top theologian gently debunks a nun's account of her 1917 vision that fueled decades of speculation.**
> **Richard Boudreaux, *Los Angeles Times*, June 27, 2000**

Evident even to a secular newspaper, Pope/Rome conclusively rejected Fatima in the Millennial Fatima Message. This is easily perceived in the June 26, 2000, official issuance of the "Fatima Message" (which was immediately followed with a June 27 "crowning" of Gorbachev at the Vatican's World Day of Peace celebration). Consequently, Catholics are, and will be, ever more intensely cursed, doomed to suffer God's apocalyptic wrath.[1]

According to Fatima, God's curse will increasingly

---

[1]

St. Thomas defines "curse" as being God's infliction of a human condition within which God allows the devils greater freedom (and, consequently, a time of greater suffering of the consequences of sin).

manifest itself physically: in wars, pestilence and other catastrophes (as well as, spiritually, in the loss of many, many souls) until the Marian Popes materialize. Only by prayer and sacrifice will the Marian Popes be brought into existence. Only then will the existential church be rePARed–brought back to par–to the God-given standard.

48

CHAPTER 6

FATIMA'S APOCALYPTIC MESSAGE SHOULD CONCERN CREDAL APOSTASY WITHIN

Pope John Paul II's inaugural encyclical, *Redemptor Hominis,* contends that *all are saved by Christ.* With God as our "most needed" Saviour set aside, the Pope assured Gorbachev, in 1989, that he dedicated the Catholic Church "to serve the cause of man and to contribute to the advance of nations" (Fatima Twilight, *Catholic Family News,* October 1995). Is it any wonder that many sensible Russian religious leaders are convinced that sympathetically dialoguing with (and, *a fortiori,* uniting with or converting to) such New Order Catholicism would constitute an act of embracing modernism of the worst kind (cf. *30 DAYS,* No. 2, 1996, p. 26)?

In response to the increasingly obvious necessity to "rePAR" the Church, Pope/Rome decided to pervert the embarrassing and increasingly relevant Fatima Message. It issued Rome's Millennial Fatima Message, which expects the faithful to believe that Russia has been converted and consecrated; the world is at peace; and that, as we enter the millennium of the New Age Order, we are entering into the promised era of Fatima Blessings.

In fact, Russia has not been properly consecrated by the Pope as Fatima demands. Consequently, Russia has not been converted to Christ-given and "Apostolic Tradition defined" Catholicism. However, the ecclesial establishment itself remains in dire need of such conversion (through vowed reparation).

A critical question arises: How can Russia be converted by an ecclesial establishment which is itself in dire need of conversion? More specifically, the reigning clergy are in dire need of conversion, since, under them, the existential church has embraced and imposed the Novus Ordo (the New Age Order) and has, thereby, apostatized from both the liturgy and dogmas of the true faith.

For ten years, the Bishop of Fatima kept an absolute silence about the content of the Third Secret. However, on September 10, 1984, Bishop do Amaral left not the slightest doubt on this subject. He tells us so in a resolute public statement presented without the slightest hesitation. According to Frere Francois de la Trinite, the Bishop consulted Sr. Lucy before stating:

> **The Secret of Fatima speaks neither of atomic bombs nor of nuclear warheads, nor of SS20 missiles. Its content concerns only our faith. To identify the Secret with catastrophic announcements or with a nuclear holocaust is to distort the meaning of the message...The Third Secret of Fatima prophesies the terrible crisis of faith from which the Church is presently suffering...The loss of faith of a continent is worse than the annihilation of a nation; and, that faith is diminishing in Europe is obviously true at the present time.**
>
> **Bishop of Fatima, Alberto Cosme do Amaral**
> ***Fatima Crusader,* Summer 2000, p. 76**

As time goes on, it becomes quite evident that the Third Secret had to predict and/or address "fiducial apostasy within." After all, we know how it begins: *"In Portugal, the dogma of the Faith will always be preserved..."* If, in Portugal, the dogma of the faith [not the liturgical morals of the faith] will be preserved, we may deduce from this, with perfect clarity, that, in other parts of the Church, fiducial dogmas will either be obscured, or else they will even be lost or denied.

Historical facts confirm the implications behind the already disclosed, very first sentence of the Third

Revelation. Among others, the following Fatima scholars have endorsed this conclusion: Fr. Alonso, Fr. Martins dos Reis, Canon Galamba, Bishop Venancio, Fr. Nicholas Gruner, Fr. Luis Kondor, and Fr. Rene Laurent.

Again and again, in her writings and communiques, Sister Lucy speaks of "false doctrines," of "diabolical delusion," of "blindness;" and this, among those very ones "who have great responsibility" in the Church. She deplores the fact that so many pastors "let themselves be swayed by the diabolical wave that is invading the world." Does this not aptly describe the crisis of a Church which glories in its having opened herself to a world of which Satan is prince?

One of the few people who have read the Third Secret has disclosed the secret as best he could. Still under the secret's spell, the top theologian of the Church informs us that the Secret concerns:

> **the dangers threatening the faith and life of the Christian... [obviously, the Canonized Mass] and therefore the world. And also the importance of the "last times."**
> **Cardinal Ratzinger, *The Ratzinger Report,* Nov. 1984**

As best he is allowed to do so, Cardinal Ratzinger assures us that Rome has lost the faith; and confirmed the great "secret" published in 1879 by Melanie herself (the seer of La Salette). Our Sorrowful Lady stated:

Rome will lose the faith and become the seat of anti-Christ.

Our Lady of La Salette

La Salette is approved prophecy. In *The Ratzinger Report* and in his other writings, has not the Prefect for the Congregation of the Doctrine of the Faith assured us that this prophecy (of an apostate existential church) has come true in our times?

The sensible among us realize that the awesome Fatima Message is being fulfilled and is yet to be fulfilled. We are in the midst of apostasy. We are in the midst of the apocalyptic battle. It is not over. We do not enjoy the promised Era of Fatima Blessings. Fatima's leading expert Fr. Joaquin Alonso, C.M.F., concluded:

> **The 1960 secret does not deal with catastrophes in the world, but primarily, with events which have occurred in the Church since the Second Vatican Council...If *'in Portugal the dogmas of the faith will always be preserved...'* it can be deduced with all clarity that in other parts of the Church these dogmas will be obscured or even lost. The message not only speaks of a 'crisis of faith' in the Church...but also makes references to internal strife among Catholics and to deficiencies of priests and religious. It implies grave *deficiencies even among the upper ranks of the hierarchy.***
>
> **Fr. Joaquin Alonso, C.M.F.**

All is as predicted by God. Over a century ago, Pope Leo XIII had an overwhelming vision of Satan's future victories. In his unabridged Leonine Prayer, Pope Leo gave greater credence to the Message of La Salette. In 1886, he ordered this prayer to be said after every Canonized (Latin) Mass Liturgy:

Archangel Michael, fight the battle of the Lord, together with the holy angels as already thou hast fought the leader of the proud angels, Lucifer, and his apostate host, who were powerless to resist thee, nor was there place for them any longer in heaven. That cruel, that ancient serpent, who is called the devil or Satan, who seduces the whole world, was cast into the abyss with his angels. Behold, this primeval enemy and slayer of men has taken courage. Transformed into an angel of light, he wanders about with all the multitude of wicked spirits, invading the earth, in order to blot out the name of God and of his Christ; to seize upon, slay and cast into eternal perdition, souls destined for the crown of eternal glory.

This wicked dragon pours out, as a most impure flood, the venom of his malice on men of depraved mind and corrupt heart, the spirit of lying, of impiety, of blasphemy, and the pestilent breath of impurity, and of every vice and iniquity. These most crafty enemies have filled and inebriated with gall and bitterness the Church, the spouse of the immaculate Lamb,

**and have laid impious hands on her most sacred
possessions. In the Holy Place itself, where has
been set up the See of the most holy Peter and
the Chair of Truth for the light of the world,
they have raised the throne of their abominable
impiety, with the iniquitous design that, when
the pastor has been struck, the sheep may be
scattered. Arise then, O invincible Prince, bring
help against the attacks of the lost spirits to the
people of God, and give them the victory.**

The Raccolta, Benziger Bros., 1930

Pope Leo XIII reinforced the Message of La Salette, as
well as, foretold the essence of the Fatima Message.
Less than fifteen years before the Fatima Message
began, Pope St. Pius X saw the big picture of the coming
apocalypse.   Soon, the New World Order would
blossom. In religion, (especially, in Novus Ordo Liturgy
as is evident today) man would be enthroned and God
would be dethroned. That which is called Russia's Errors
by Our Lady was foreseen as *"this monstrous and
detestable iniquity"* by Pope Pius X.

> **We understood that it belonged to Us, in virtue
> of the pontifical office entrusted to Us, to
> provide a remedy for such a great evil [apostasy
> from God]. We believed that this order of God
> was addressed to Us: 'Behold, today I set you
> over nations and kingdoms, to tear down and
> destroy, to build up and to plant' (Jer 1,10)...It is
> necessary, by every means, and at the price of
> any effort, to uproot entirely *this monstrous and***

detestable iniquity proper to the times we are living in, and through which man substitutes himself for God. We must necessarily and firmly fear whether such a perversion of minds is not the sign announcing, and the beginning of the last times, and that the Son of Perdition spoken of by the Apostle (11Thess 2,3) might already be living on this earth....

Now this, according to the Apostle, is the character proper to Antichrist; man, with unspeakable temerity, has usurped the place of the Creator, lifting himself above everything that bears the name of God. It has reached such a point that, being powerless to completely extinguish in himself the notion of God, he nevertheless shakes off the yoke of His Majesty, and dedicates the visible world to himself in the guise of the temple, where he pretends to receive the adoration of his own kind... *"He sits in the temple of God, and gives himself out as if he were God"* (II Thess 2,4).
Pope St. Pius X, *E Supremi Apostolatus Cathedra, (From My Supreme Apostolic Throne)*

CHAPTER 7

THE APOCALYPTIC FATIMA MESSAGE SHOULD CONCERN LITURGICAL APOSTASY WITHIN

There shall be offered in the churches no more Oblation, nor incense, nor worship acceptable to God.
St. Hippolytus, quote, Card. Manning, *Crisis of the Holy See*

Besides Fatima's prediction of fiducial apostasy, one is led to conclude that Fatima also predicted, presumed or addressed an unprecedented internal liturgical apostasy which is all too evident in our Novus Ordo times. Most of the world is enveloped in both fiducial and liturgical apostasy. Cardinal Manning (in *Crisis of the Holy See)* showed that all of the Church Fathers predicted a time during which Holy Mass would no longer exist.

Popes Predict/Confirm Liturgical Apostasy Within

Recall the vision of Pope Leo XIII a century ago. This vision led him to compose his Leonine Prayer. This previously cited prayer contained the following pertinent paragraph:

> **In the Holy Place itself, where has been set up the See of the most holy Peter and the Chair of Truth for the Light of the world, they have raised the throne of their abominable impiety, with the iniquitous design that when the Pastor has been struck, the sheep will scatter... [and thus, leave the flock of Christ].**
> *The Raccolta*, **Benziger Bros., 1930, p. 314**

"Abominable impiety" indicates that apostasy within will be liturgical! The source and summit of all piety, the Mass, will be sacrileged into "abominable impiety" from and by "the throne of *papal* impiety." So did Pope Leo XIII predict. So has it been fulfilled. A few years later, almost a century ago, God gave us Pope Saint Pius X. He also predicted (what subsequently materialized as) the Novus Ordo (New World Order) Liturgy:

> **Man, with unspeakable temerity, has usurped the place of the Creator, lifting himself above everything that bears the name of God. It has reached such a point that, being powerless to completely extinguish in himself the notion of**

God, he nevertheless shakes off the yoke of His Majesty, and dedicates the visible world to himself in the guise of the temple, where he pretends to receive the adoration of his own kind...'He sits in the temple of God, and gives himself out as if he were God (IIThes.2,4).'
E Supremi Apostolatus Cathedra, Pope Pius X, Oct. 4, 1903

This spirit (the spirit condemned by Pope St. Pius X) is clearly manifested in the establishment's official directive which insists that every eucharistic minister of the bread (sic) address (by looking into his face and not at the "bread") each potential communicant with the words "Body of Christ." Only when the communicant boldly affirms "Amen" (that he/she is, indeed, the "Body of Christ") is he/she to be rewarded with a "eucharistic wafer" sacrilegiously placed into his/her outstretched hand. Only a few years before Vatican II, Pope Pius XII made an amazing prediction concerning the Novus Ordo Liturgy, the most rotten fruit of the "spirit of Vatican II:"

I am worried by the Blessed Virgin's messages to Lucy of Fatima. This persistence of Mary about the dangers which menace the Church is a divine warning *against the suicide of altering the Faith in her liturgy.*[Obviously, by introducing, tolerating and imposing Novus Ordo Services] A day will come when the civilized world will deny its God, *when the Church will doubt as Peter doubted.* She will be tempted to

believe that man has become God. In our churches, Christians *will search in vain for the red lamp* where God awaits them. Like Mary Magdalene, weeping before the empty tomb, they will ask, "Where have they taken Him?"

Inside the Vatican, Jan. 1997, p. 7, quoting Msgr. Roche, "Pie XII devant l' histoire," pp. 52-53.

Has not the existential church "self-destructed" or committed suicide in altering the Catholic Faith by mutating the liturgy? Has not Christ vacated Himself from Novus Ordo tabernacles? From key papal confessions such as this, one is led to conclude that the Third Revelation of Fatima addresses the Novus Ordo liturgical sacrilege, directly or indirectly.

In stating: *"Catholics would search in vain for the red [sanctuary] lamp"* Pope Pius XII confirmed the basic message of the Church-approved apparition of Our Lady (as Our Lady of Good Fortune) to a nun in Quito, Ecuador, on February 2, 1634. The visible essence of this Marian apparition was the miraculous extinguishing of the sanctuary lamp while she was in adoration before the tabernacle. This extinguishing prefigured the absence of Christ in the "Holy Eucharist" and in the church's sanctuaries.

Liturgical Apostasy Indeed!

A continuing and ever growing sacrilegious attitude is implied by the word *"apostasy."* As predicted by Pope Leo XIII, and according to his prayer, Church liturgy would be sacrileged. Pope John XXIII (in his Apostolic Constitution *Veterum Sapientiae)* recognized vernacularization as tantamount to liturgical apostasy. In this solemn decree, he bound the bishops *"to be on their guard lest anyone under their jurisdiction"* speak up or write against the canonized Latin Liturgy, or in his exact words: *"the use of Latin in the Liturgy"* (www.traditio.com, Papal Photo Gallery).

Christ gave us the Holy Sacrifice. His Church precisely canonized its form (words). Since 1966, the upper clergy have imposed upon us, blasphemous liturgical sacrilege.

Even Pope Paul VI confessed that he had created and imposed a sacrilegious "novelty," which removed the Holy Sacrifice of apostolic tradition. He did so, that man may be glorified–so that laymen may "have a supernatural conversation with God;" ultimately, so that laymen can celebrate or say "Mass." He stated:

> **A new rite of the mass...affects our hereditary patrimony which [up until now] seemed to be untouchable and settled...We are giving up**

**something of priceless worth...pious people will
be disturbed...this _novelty_ is no small thing...**
[We now implement a service] **which shows that
the faithful are qualified to have a supernatural
conversation with God.**
Pope Paul VI, November 26, 1969

Pope Paul VI "gave up" Christ. In place of the Christ-given and Church-canonized Liturgy, he imposed a sacrilegious novelty that led him to confess: _"The [incense] smoke of_ [our liturgically worshiping] _Satan is in our sanctuary."_ The Second (Novus Ordo) Beast worships Man (666) and thereby worships Satan (Apoc 13). This landmark papal confession indicates that Novus Ordo Liturgical Services have grossly sacrileged the Christ-given Mass Liturgy (sacrileged to such an extent that it became a legion of Satan-worshiping services).

How could Fatima's Third Secret ignore such a fact, disclosed by the Pope himself? How could Fatima's Third Secret possibly "upstage" such a papal disclosure? Must it not somehow address, build upon or assume this papal confession of liturgical apostasy?

> **Your sons ask for Bread of faith and no one gives It to them...Ungrateful Rome, effeminate Rome, arrogant Rome...forgetting that the Sovereign Pontiff's and your true glory are on Golgotha...Woe to you.**
> _The Memoires,_ St. John Bosco

Rome's glory is the Holy Sacrifice (not a happy meal). Rome's glory is Golgotha (not a pleasant protestantized commemoration of the past).

The Latin Rite Patriarchate's glory is the Canonized Latin Mass Liturgy, not a "manipulated" and "intellectually and morally relative" [relative to each fallen man's desires] cacophony of Novus Ordo mass-like services. Even Pope John Paul II confesses the sacrilegious "novelty" of the New Order Services:

> **Veritable heresies have been propagated in the areas of dogma and morals** [liturgical as well as personal and social] **creating doubt, confusion and rebellion...The liturgy has been manipulated...it has plunged into intellectual and moral relativism...Everything is allowed.**
> **Pope John Paul II, *L'Osservatore Romano*, Feb. 8, 1981**

Strangest of all, the establishment itself admits the truth. Novus Ordo mass-like services were manipulated or created by man–specifically, and initially, by the freemason, apostate priest, Bugnini, with the approval of heretical protestant ministers:

> **The liturgical reform has made remarkable progress in the ecumenical domain and has drawn nearer to the liturgical forms of the Lutheran church."**
> ***Osservatore Romano*, October 13, 1967**

Is it not a sad day in Catholicism when the official Catholic paper boasts about the establishment using heretical protestant Mass-mocking liturgies? The imposition of liturgical heresy did not go unnoticed. Cardinals Ottaviani and Bacci drew the attention of Pope Paul VI to the outstanding sacrilegious nature of the Novus Ordo:

> **The Novus Ordo represents, both as a whole and in its details, a striking departure from the Catholic theology of the Mass.**
> **Confession of Augsbourg and of Lorrain, December 8, 1973**

In other words, the Novus Ordo departed from the Canonized Liturgy to such an extent that it replaced the Catholic religion with a Protestant heretical religion. Protestantism did away with the Priesthood and the Sacrifice of the Altar. It made the preacher the center of Protestant worship, and threw out all statues, painting, etc. The fruit of the Second Vatican Council is the creation and imposition of liturgical Protestantism within the Catholic Church.

The Third Secret, *cannot but* presume or address liturgical apostasy within. Any and all proposals for a "relevantly prophetic" Third Revelation of Fatima, which fail to do so, should be dismissed as incredible.

How can the Fatima Message, which began and climaxed "with" Holy Mass (the Canonized Mass Liturgy) contain a Third Secret, which does not in some way address or correct the gross sacrilege of Holy Mass—the Novus Ordo Mass-mocking sacrilegious services? Recall Fatima's beginning in the spring of 1916:

> **Leaving the chalice suspended in the air, the Angel prostrated beside us and made us repeat three times:**
>
> **My God, I believe, I adore, I hope, I love Thee! I ask pardon for those who do not believe, do not adore, do not hope in and do not love Thee.**
>
> **Most Holy Trinity, Father, Son and Holy Ghost, I adore Thee profoundly!**
>
> **I offer Thee the most precious Body, Blood, Soul and Divinity of our Lord and Saviour, Jesus Christ, present in all the tabernacles throughout the world, in reparation for all the outrages, sacrileges and indifferences with which He Himself is offended.**
>
> **Through the infinite merits of His Most Sacred Heart and the Immaculate Heart of Mary** [Holy Mass, as Tuy would disclose], **I pray for the conversion of poor sinners.**
>
> Prayer given by the Angel of Peace, Fatima 1916

To silence forever the "blind, faithful-to-the-company men" (those who refuse to see or even hold as a possibility that the Novus Ordo mass-like services are totally invalid) as far back as 1861, Cardinal Manning saw very clearly that the cessation of the Holy Mass was coming, having read carefully the writings of the Fathers on this subject from the earliest times. This great Cardinal gives us the following inspired predictions:

> **The Holy Fathers who have written upon the subject of antichrist, and of the prophecies of Daniel, without a single exception, as far as I know–and they are the Fathers both of the East and of the West, the Greek and the Latin Church–all of them unanimously–say that in the latter end of the world, during the reign of Antichrist, the Holy Sacrifice of the altar will cease. In the work on the end of the world, ascribed to St. Hippolytus, after a long description of the afflictions of the last days, we read as follows:**

> **The Churches shall lament with a great lamentation, for there shall be offered no more oblation nor worship acceptable to God. The sacred buildings of the churches shall be as hovels; and the precious Body and Blood of Christ shall not be manifest in those days; the true Liturgy shall become extinct...Such is the universal testimony of the Fathers of the early centuries.**
> **Cardinal Manning, *Crisis of the Holy See*, 1861**

In addition to Cardinal Manning, the German mystic, Anna Catherina Emmerich (1774-1824), had visions and mystical experiences in which she saw the birth of what she terms "the dark church" and "the black counterfeit church." The word "counterfeit" denotes more than just the idea of false. (There have been many false churches.) "Counterfeit" implies deliberate deception.

> **They did not receive the Body of the Lord, but only bread. They were in error through no fault of their own and those who piously and ardently longed for the Body of Jesus Christ were spiritually consoled; but not by their communion. They who habitually communicated without this ardent love received nothing.**
> *Life of Anna Catherina Emmerich,* **Very Rev. Schmoeger, 1867, pp. 85 & 132**

CHAPTER 8

THE THIRD SECRET MUST PRESUME AND ADDRESS GOD'S JUST WRATH

When men are not ruled by God, they will soon be crushed by tyrants. Where they do not bend the knee in prayer, they will at last bend the back in slavery.
William Penn

Such, basically, is God's "relational law" with mankind. Do evil; be punished. According to St. Pius X, today man is so wicked that he has put himself in the place of God. Obviously, God's "Sodom-like" wrath" has been postponed, not averted. God's just wrath is inevitable.

The Church will be [is now] eclipsed and the world will be [is now] in consternation.
Our Lady of La Salette

The Third Secret must assure us that those who expect God's wrath to increase until the coming of the glorious Marian Pope are correct for doing so. On the other hand, Rome's Millennial Fatima Message would have one believe that God's wrath is over because company churchmen assure us that the church now confidently marches into the millennial New Age, the Novus Ordo Saeclorum.

Since the first and last sentences of the Third Secret have already been revealed, one can reasonably conjecture what is missing from the Third Revelation. The dogma and liturgy of the faith were weakened or destroyed outside of Portugal, and *"in the end, my Immaculate Heart will triumph"* indicate that the authentic Third Revelation must refer to God's wrath.

This wrath was not accomplished and terminated when the Pope (John Paul II) was "killed and not killed," as Pope/Rome's millennial Fatima propaganda (of May-June 2000) contends. In fact, the establishment insulted, blasphemed and sacrileged Holy Mary (in its Millennial Fatima Message). Realistically, one awaits God's greater wrath, not Fatima's blessings.

While living within and subjected to the current confusing neo-Hegelian ecclesial powers, one might ask which Pope John Paul II one might follow: the millennial optimist—or—the 1980 realist? The 1980 Pope gave us a glimpse of the coming horrors in store for Fatima-rejecting mankind. In 1980, a German newspaper ran this thought-provoking and startling response to the German pilgrims at Fulda who asked him to disclose the Third Secret:

> 'It should have been made public in 1960, but because of its troubling content, and to dissuade the superpowers from undertaking war, my predecessors in the papal chair have chosen the diplomatic way.' The Pope thus admitted the authenticity of the excerpt made by Pope Paul VI. 'All Christians should be content in the knowledge that the oceans will inundate whole continents, and millions of people will die from one moment to the next. Hearing this, people should not long for the rest of the secret.
>
> We should prepare for trials in the near future. We should be prepared to lose our lives. We must give ourselves completely to Christ and for Christ! That the great curses or trials can be mitigated by them is no longer possible, because only in this way can the real renewal of the Church come about. How often the Church has been renewed in blood! It won't be otherwise now.'
>
> *Stimme Des Glaubens,* **Fall, 1980**

The Nature of God's Wrath

Does this sound familiar? Sister Lucy assured us concerning the Third Secret: *"It's in the Gospel and in the Apocalypse, read them."* The Bible demands harsh punishments for such wicked times. Blessed Anna Maria Taigi wrote of the coming chastisement, saying:

> **God will ordain two punishments: One in the form of wars, revolutions and other evils, will originate on earth; the other, will be sent from heaven. There shall come over all the earth an intense darkness lasting three days and three nights...the air will be laden with pestilence, which will claim principally, but not exclusively, the enemies of religion.**
> **Blessed Anna Maria Taigi, † 1837**

The greatest wickedness in our times is, as Sister Lucy stated: *"The clergy are diabolically disoriented."* La Salette (September 19, 1846) confirmed this: *"God will strike in an unprecedented way...The Church will witness a frightful crisis."*

Sister Lucy spells out this frightful crisis: She speaks of "false doctrines," of "diabolical confusion," of "blindness," and this among those very ones "who have great responsibility" in the Church. She deplores the fact that so many pastors "let themselves be swayed by the

72

diabolical wave that is invading the world." Paradoxically, God's greatest punishment is granting us the evil clergymen we deserve.

> **The churches will be deprived of God-fearing and pious pastors...most will lose their faith... They will lack even the opportunity of seeing the [salutary] truth.**
>
> St. Nilus, 430

> **The churches will be closed or profaned...Many will give up the faith, and the number of priests and religious who will dissociate themselves from the true religion will be great; among them there will be bishops.**
>
> Our Lady of La Salette

> **The thesis of the late lamented (†12 December 1981) Father Joaquin Alonso (the only official expert), so embarrassing for Rome, proved that the Third Secret foretold the blindness, the disorientation and the apostasy of the pastors and of the popes themselves.**
>
> *Catholic Counter-Revolution,* p. 15, Aug. 1997

> **Over the flock and over the shepherds, My hand will weigh heavy. Famine, pestilence and war will be such that mothers will have to cry on account of the blood of their sons and of their martyrs dead in a hostile world.**
>
> *The Memoires,* St. John Bosco, 1888

Jesus told Padre Pio, 'Pray and make reparation to Me. Admonish others to do the same because the time is near at hand in which I shall visit my unfaithful people because they have not heeded the time of My grace. Persevere in prayer, so that your adversary shall have no dominion over you...I shall protect the just and punish the wicked.
Words of Our Lord to Padre Pio, Dec. 31, 1949. Letter from Padre Pio, addressed to the Commission of Heroldsbach

The Fatima Apocalypse is now! The unveiling of apocalyptic horrors is just beginning.

The good will be martyred, the Holy Father will have much to suffer, various nations will be annihilated.
Our Lady of Fatima

CHAPTER 9

THE THIRD SECRET MUST CONCERN THE MARTYRED MARIAN POPE

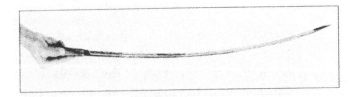

Suddenly, the Pope falls, seriously wounded. He is instantly helped up, but struck a second time, dies. But no sooner is the Pope dead than another takes his place...the new Pope guides the ship right up to the two columns and comes to rest between them; he makes it fast with a light chain that hangs from the bow to an anchor of the column on which stands the Host; and with another light chain which hangs from the stern, he fastens it at the opposite end to another anchor hanging from the column on which stands the Immaculate Virgin.
St. John Bosco, May 30, 1862

The vision of St. John Bosco complements the Fatima Message. This vision assures us that two Marian Popes will be brought into existence by our prayers and sacrifices. One will suffer and be martyred. The other will be glorious in victory.

A pertinent prediction was made by Blessed Pius IX, who was often inspired (in his public speeches) by the two secrets of La Salette. In 1871, on the 25th anniversary of his election, he said to a French deputation presided over by Mgr. Forcade of Nevers:

> **There will be a great wonder that will astonish the whole world. This wonder, however, has to be preceded by the triumph of the Revolution. The Church will have much to suffer: her ministers and head first and foremost will be dishonored, persecuted and martyred.**
> **Pope Pius IX, 1871**

Such a suffering and martyred Marian Pope was also predicted by Pope St. Pius X in one of his visions:

> **I saw one of my successors taking to flight over the bodies of his brethren. He will die a cruel death. The present wickedness of the world is only the beginning of the sorrows which must take place before the end of the world.**
> **Yves Dupont, *Catholic Prophecy,* The Coming Chastisement, p.22**

CHAPTER 10

THE MYSTERY OF SALVATION
HOLY MASS AND HOLY MARY

They [Holy Mary's Remnant] **overcome the enemy by the Blood of the Lamb.**
Apocalypse 12:11

Holy Mass, the Holy Sacrifice, saves and sanctifies. Mary's Remnant have become convinced by God's providential interventions in modern history: that Holy Mary and Holy Mass are essential constituents of the Mystery of Salvation. Therefore, God's apocalyptic message concerns the restoration of devotion to Holy Mary and Holy Mass. Fatima makes this explicit in stating that God wishes to place devotion to the Immaculate Heart (of Holy Mary) alongside devotion to the Sacred Heart of Jesus (the Mass).

At Tuy, Fatima reveals the deep urgency of retaining the Holy Sacrifice of Mass within the Latin Rite. Holy Mary has come down to earth to tell us that, without the Holy Sacrifice, Christ (Holy Sacrament) is not sacramentally present among us. Tuy also reflects that Holy Mary is used mystically by the Holy Ghost to confect Holy Mass (as St. Maximilian Kolbe disclosed).

To convince us that Holy Mass is God's greatest gift and our greatest need, Our Lady of the Canonized Mass came among us (in the patriarchate of the Canonized Latin Mass Rite) as: Our Lady of Guadalupe; Our Lady of the Miraculous Medal; Our Lady of Pontmain; Our Lady of La Salette; Our Lady of Lourdes; Our Lady of Knock; Our Lady of Fatima; as well as, many other lesser-known private visitations to sainted or saintly persons.

Indeed, Our Lady has come to Latin Rite Catholics over the past five hundred or so years as Our Lady of the Canonized (Latin) Mass. How did Our Lady indicate this in all of her major visitations? All Church-approved Marian visitations within the Latin Rite (since 1500) demanded that chapels (churches) be built for the celebration of the Canonized Mass Liturgy; or, they have occurred within and emphasized such churches and their Canonized Masses.

Only in such places can Holy Mary "birth her children."[1] Only in such places can proper and adequate devotion to the Two Hearts exist in our space-time continuum.

Only through Holy Mass does Holy Mary conceive, nurture and offer the Elect as "victims to God." Holy Mass defines the Immaculata. Each Holy Mass is the "salutary doing" of the Two Hearts; and, of the Elect's "salutary doing" through and in the Two Hearts.

> **The most August Heart of the Mother of God is the temple in which the victims of love are sacrificed. Who are these victims? They are of three principal kinds: The first is that adorable Victim whom the Blessed Virgin offered to God with all her Heart and with an inconceivable love in the temple of Jerusalem and on Calvary, and Whom she continues to offer in Heaven and in all the divine sacrifices which are made every day and at every hour throughout the world...**
>
> **The second victim who is sacrificed in this same temple is she herself, the Mother of the Saviour...The third victim** [the Elect or Mary's Remnant] **comprises the countless number who have been, are and will be sacrificed to God in the marvelous temple of this virginal Heart.**
> **St. John Eudes**

[1] Pope St. Pius X (in *Ad Diem Illum*, Feb. 2, 1904) confirmed a great mystery: "As Mary carried Jesus in her womb, it is said that Mary also carried all those whose lives were included in the life of the Saviour."

Each Holy Mass is the Mystery of Faith enacted in our midst. At Calvary, as at each valid Mass, the Holy Ghost, through Holy Mother Mary, as it were, conceives and births Jesus and the Elect. Also, at each valid Canonized Mass, the Holy Ghost (through Holy Mary) sustains or nourishes each of the Elect, especially, who fervently pray the Holy Mass and devoutly receive the Holy Sacrament. Through Holy Mass now, and eternally in Heaven, the Holy Ghost glorifies the Elect.

At each valid Canonized Mass, the Holy Ghost, through Holy Mary and her priest, transubstantiates or metamorphosizes each Christ-sacrificed human life into one of the Elect just as He (the Holy Ghost) through Holy Mary and her priest metamorphosizes bread and wine into Holy Sacrifice and, thereby, Holy Sacrament. Holy Mary's children, the Elect, are mystically born on earth, only as the Sacred Heart is once again made present (sacramentally, yet substantially) on earth by the words of validly functioning priests. Holy Mary and Holy Mass are thus one.

On earth, only at Holy Mass is devotion to the Immaculate Heart of Mary properly and fully placed alongside devotion to the Sacred Heart of Jesus. Here and here alone is the Our Father realized: "God's Saving Will is done on earth as it is done in Heaven, by Christ, through His handmaiden and through His and her priest."

Our Lady of the Canonized Mass

 Our Lady of Guadalupe began our modern times and (so far, at least) the "tilma portrait"of Our Lady remains with us in mid-America. Her message continues to be validated. The miraculous nature of Guadalupe was further confirmed recently by means of the use of the technique of digital imagery, which disclosed a family present "within" the right iris of Our Lady of Guadalupe. Our Lady's special gift is given to us at a time when the family remains under serious attack in our modern world.[1]

In 1531, Our Lady appeared as Our Lady of the Apocalypse (Apoc 12). She appeared clothed with the sun (Apoc 12:1). Her black ribbon indicated she was pregnant with Child (Apoc 12:2). She came to defeat Satan (Apoc 12:3). As in Genesis (ch. 3), so at Mexico City and throughout the Americas, Our Lady conquers Satan, the snake, who writhes under her feet. She conquers Satan through birthing and sacrificing her Child, both at Bethlehem, as well as, at every Canonized Mass Liturgy.

---

[1]

See *Catholic,* February 2001.

To do so, Our Lady requested that a traditional or canonical temple (a "teocalli") be built and that Canonized Masses be said; in order, as it were, to once again birth Holy Sacrament and the Elect among us. By her establishment of chapels for the celebration of the Mass throughout the land, Our Lady was able to accomplish the cessation of the cult of human sacrifice. When Our Lady's Fatima requests are fulfilled and the Holy Canonized Mass Liturgy is once more restored to Christ's Church, will not the apostasy of the present day cult of human sacrifice (abortion on demand) cease?

Holy Mass Has Two Hearts

Our Lady blessed France with the greatest number of major Marian apparitions of modern times. In 1830, at Rue du Bac, St. Catherine Laboure received the Miraculous Medal from the Immaculata, who came to her in the Sanctuary, where the Sacred Heart was tabernacled among us.

Have a medal struck according to this model. Everyone who wears it with confidence will receive great graces.
Our Lady to St. Catherine Laboure

This medal is referred to us as the Miraculous Medal. On the front is the image of the Blessed Virgin, her outstretched hands emitting rays symbolic of graces obtained by those who ask for them. Around the outer edge of the Medal is the prayer: *"O Mary, conceived without sin, pray for us who have recourse to thee!"*

Then, it seemed to Saint Catherine that the frame was turned over, presenting in its center the letter M, surmounted by a cross with a bar at its base, a symbol of the altar on which the Sacrifice of the Cross is perpetuated. Below were the two Hearts of Jesus and Mary, the first surrounded by a crown of thorns, the second pierced by a sword. This medal also "signs" the union of the Sacred Heart and the Immaculate Heart in Holy Mass. Thereby, God emphasized that Holy Mass has Two Hearts.

> **Tell everybody that God grants us graces through the Immaculate Heart of Mary; that people are to ask her for them; and that the Heart of Jesus wants the Immaculate Heart of Mary to be venerated at His side.**
> *Fatima in Lucia's Own Words*, pp. 111-112

"The Heart of Jesus wants the Immaculate Heart of Mary to be venerated at His side" on earth. The Heart of Jesus wants the worldwide restoration of the Canonized Mass Liturgy. Fatima and all other modern Marian apparitions "in the west," as it were, cry out "Bring back

and pray God's greatest Gift to men on earth: the Canonized Mass Liturgy."

Such a divinely urgent message culminates with the Canonized Mass Salutary Theophany at Tuy. As with the God-dictated Miraculous Medal, this greatest salutary theophany of all times shows the Two Hearts as "constituting the Salutary Sacrifice." Grace and mercy come from the Canonized Mass or from the Sacred Heart of Jesus through the Immaculate Heart of our Mother in Heaven. As Sister Lucy says so well:

> **I always remember the great promise (of Our Lady) which fills me with joy: *'I will never forsake you. My Immaculate Heart will be your refuge and the way that will lead you to God.'***
>
> **I believe that this promise is not for me alone, but for all those souls who wish to take refuge in the Heart of their heavenly Mother and allow themselves to be led along the paths...by her.**
> **Letter,14 April 1945, pp. 62-63, *Fatima Coracao de Maria*, Fr. A.M. Martins, S.J.**

Build a Church

A few years after Our Lady appeared in Paris, she came to La Salette and commanded that a church be built on that site. However, she went beyond God's positive message to disclose the existential church's "negative dimension," (which is both the cause and effect of the loss of Holy Mass among us). She warned that the clergy, especially, the uppermost clergy, would insult Jesus Christ and blaspheme her, His Mother (even as "her church" at La Salette is now sacrileged and blasphemed by Novus Ordo services).

 Appearing to Maximin Giraud (age 11) and Melanie Calvat (age 15) at La Salette, Our Lady wept. She focused on the main danger facing the church–unworthy or evil priests, bishops and popes. She warns us not to put them before (or in the place of) God and His Salutary Will.

Rome will lose the Faith and become the seat of anti-christ...The Church will be in eclipse.
Our Lady of La Salette

Every authentic apparition is validated. Melanie's signs of validation are that she was a stigmatist from an early age; she worked miracles; and she made short-term predictions which came true during her lifetime. (See *Melanie* and *Sister Mary of the Cross,* available from MAETA.) Melanie was uniquely bonded to the Holy Sacrifice and Holy

Sacrament. She lived for long periods without food. Her only food was the Fruit of the Holy Sacrifice, the Holy Eucharist. Holy Mary challenged Melanie and Maximin to be her Apostles of the Latter Times:

> **Go, show yourselves as my beloved children: I am with you and in you, provided that your faith be the light that enlightens you in these days of woe. May your zeal cause you to be famished for the glory and honor of Jesus Christ. Fight, children of light, you little number who see clearly. For behold, the time of times, the end of ends.**
>
> **Blessed Virgin to Melanie,** *The Secret of La Salette*

Build a Chapel

What was the message to Bernadette in 1858? *"Build a chapel here!"* Build a chapel for the celebration of the Canonized Mass. Only at and through Holy Mass is Holy Mary properly reverenced.

Before the revolting sixties, more than two million people visited Lourdes each year. Some were cured as Christ, the Holy Sacrament, was raised over them in benediction. Others were cured as they received Christ, the Holy Sacrament. And, still others were cured at the

Holy Sacrifice. Always, these miracles occurred at Holy Mass and/or in the presence of the Holy Sacrament, born of Holy Mary and of the Holy Sacrifice.

When given up for dying on April 30, 1862, St. Bernadette, upon receiving the Holy Sacrament, was cured instantly. Along with the great saints, her life was one of prayer and sacrifice, offered on behalf of sinners; offered as united to the Holy Sacrifice of the Mass.

In the beginning, Bernadette's pastor had reservations. In those days, priests were pastors and shepherds, not subservient community facilitators and empty-headed episcopal collaborators. Our Lady gave Monsieur L'Abbe Peyramale the proof of authenticity which he sought, regarding the visions at Massabielle. As he fed his flock, as he gave them Christ, Holy Sacrament, a spectacular luminous halo drew him to a young girl. He gave her Holy Communion. Later on, he realized that she was Bernadette Soubirous. After that, he wholeheartedly supported her. This information is reported in a deposition for the canonization of St. Bernadette.

As shown in the salutary Tuy apparition of Fatima, miraculous water represents the grace and mercy given by the Holy Sacrifice. To confirm the authenticity of La Salette, (as well as Lourdes) water miraculously sprung forth by Our Lady's command. All of these observations concerning modern Marian visitations are presented to impress upon our minds that God (in all of His modern apparitions) has come to convince us that Holy Mass and Holy Mary are His greatest gifts to mankind.

The Altar of the Lamb

In the Church in County Mayo, Ireland, on August 21, 1879, St. Joseph and St. John appeared, within the Mass–with the Crucifix and the Altar of the Lamb. This

Mass-theophany connected Heaven with earth. It connected the Holy Mass on earth with Heaven's eternal Mass. It demonstrated that God's Saving Will done on earth was identical to His Saving Will done in Heaven.

The Lamb of the Apocalypse defines Heaven (Apoc 4). This is the Sacrifice Lamb of the Canonized Mass. This is Heaven's unending Mass. This is the Holy Sacrifice of the Mass–God's effective Salutary Will, *"done on earth as it is in Heaven."*

This shrine was approved by the Holy See. It is frequented by over a million visitors each year. Here, Our Lady of the Canonized Mass is no longer honored as such. Without Holy Mass, Holy Mary cannot be properly and fully honored. Unfortunately, the Holy Mass that Holy Mary "apparitioned" is no longer celebrated at Knock.

90

CHAPTER 11

TUY CONFIRMS THE MASS AS THE SALUTARY DOING OF THE TWO HEARTS

From its inception to its climax, the Fatima Message focused upon the Canonized Mass and Holy Mary as Our Lady of the Canonized Mass. In 1916, the Angel brought Holy Communion to the children of Fatima (most likely, from Padre Pio's Mass, since only a valid priest, not even an angel, can consecrate or "confect" the Eucharist).

The climax of the Fatima Message occurred in Tuy, Spain in 1929. This Canonized Mass Salutary Theophany, showed that Holy Mass and Holy Mary are the Triune God's greatest Gifts to us sinners.

While praying during a Holy Hour in the chapel at Tuy, Sister Lucy of Fatima had a vision far more spectacular than the theophany to Moses on Mount Sinai; and comparable to Christ's theophany to His selected apostles (the Transfiguration on Mount Tabor).

On June 13, 1929, Sister Lucy experienced this great theophany. She left us a brief description of her experience of the Holy Mass and Holy Mary. Before the Blessed Sacrament, she recited, again and again, the Mass-centered prayers given to her by God's angel in 1916, at Fatima, Portugal. In Sister Lucy's own words:

> **Suddenly, a supernatural light illumined the whole chapel; and, on the altar, appeared a cross of light, which reached to the ceiling. In a brighter part could be seen, on the upper part of the Cross, the face of a man and His body to the waist. On His breast was an equally luminous dove, and nailed to the Cross, the body of another man.**
>
> **A little below the waist, suspended in midair, was to be seen a Chalice and a large Host onto which fell some drops of Blood from the face of the Crucified, and from a wound in His breast. These drops ran down over the Host and fell into the Chalice.**
>
> **Under the right arm of the Cross was Our Lady, with her Immaculate Heart in her hand...**

It was Our Lady of Fatima with her Immaculate Heart...in her left hand...without a sword or roses, but with a crown of thorns and flames.

Under the left arm (of the Cross) some big letters, as it were, of crystal clear water running down over the Altar, formed these words: 'Grace and Mercy.'

I understood that it was the Mystery of the Most Holy Trinity that was shown to me, and I received lights about this Mystery, which I am not permitted to reveal.
The Whole Truth About Fatima, Frere Michael, Vol. 2.
Available from Fatima Crusader 1-800-263-8160

The Virgin Mary has *both the active and the passive creature part* in the Mystery of Faith, the Mystery of Salvation through Christ Jesus. As active, Holy Mary is co-redemptrix. As passive, she alone is the Immaculate One who "attracted God to open Heaven to her;" to forgive the sins of her Christ-bestowed children (the Elect); and, to open Heaven to them, as well.

We are in the age of the Holy Ghost. The Holy Ghost applies salvation through Holy Mass and Holy Mary, the only perfect and sinless human person.

"Hail, Mary, the channel of graces (full of grace)..." as the original Greek strongly implies and clearly means.

Holy Mary channels the salutary graces of Holy Mass (Christ/Holy Ghost) to the Elect. Our Lady of the Canonized Mass is integral to the Salutary Canonized Mass Theophany of Fatima's Tuy. God wills it to be so. Sister Lucy tells us this when she assured us regarding this theophany:

> **I understood that I had been shown the Mystery of the Holy Trinity.**
> **Sister Lucy of Fatima, regarding the Theophany of Tuy**

In order to be saved from Hell, one must never blaspheme Holy Mary. One must never despise or question God's freely willed favoring of Holy Mary. Instead, one should venerate the Immaculate thorn-pierced Heart of Mary in the conviction that, as one does so, he venerates, appreciates and thanks God for Holy Mass and Holy Church—the only hope for escaping from Hell.

Holy Mary is the uniquely active human person who helped bring about salvation. If one of us can be active in salvation (according to the Colossians' Mystery, Col 1:25) how much infinitely more so is the Immaculata, who alone (by God's grace and her graced cooperation) is perfectly divinely feminine to God or "perfectly submissive to (and thus, transparent to) the Holy Trinitarian economy of salvation?"

CHAPTER 12

PRIEST-PATRIARCHS OF THE FUTURE APOCALYPTIC ARMY OF MARIAN PRIESTS

Since Holy Mary and Holy Mass are united and characterize the only Church of salvation, it is to be expected that validly ordained, properly-facultied and "Canonized Mass Liturgy praying" priests should have a special role in these Fatima-predicted, Apocalyptic times. Indeed such is the case.

Already, the future is foreshadowed in these forerunners of the great army of patriarchical Marian priests. Some of these outstanding patriarchical priest-saints who were characterized by special devotion to Holy Mary and Holy Mass are St. Padre Pio, St. Maximilian Kolbe, St. Louis de Montford and St. John Bosco.

Padre Pio, the only priest stigmatist, (being one of the last priests who exclusively prayed the Canonized Mass Latin Liturgy) merits the title of the priest-saint of the Canonized Mass. His three-hour Canonized Latin Masses were prayed so intently that he *"became Holy Mass"* in as much as such is possible for a Marian priest.

Being blind for the last five years of his priestly life, it was not possible for him to say any other Mass prayers but those of the Canonized Latin Mass Liturgy in honor of the Immaculate Conception —even after the Novus Ordo Services were officially imposed. Padre Pio's devotion to Holy Mary is unrivaled. Each day, he recited thirty to fifty entire rosaries. With the rosary, he lived on the altar all day long. Padre Pio's devotion to Holy Mass and Holy Mary is epitomized by the altar and the rosary.

Love Our Lady and make others love her. Recite the rosary always and well. Satan aims always at destroying this form of prayer, but he will never succeed. It is the prayer leading to Him Who triumphs over everything and everybody. She [Mary] was the one who teaches us [the rosary] just as Jesus has taught us the "Our Father."

Padre Pio

Fr. Maximilian Kolbe was entirely devoted to the Immaculata. He was also especially devoted to Fatima.

> **Our love for the Immaculata must be such that it consumes both our soul and our body. The soul in which burns the fire of this love consumes itself for her. From this arises the sacrifice of suffering and prayer. The soul which gives itself to the Immaculata loves true suffering.**
>
> **St. Maximilian Kolbe**

In February of 1937, Maximilian Kolbe gave a conference in Rome. At this time, he gave this encouraging prophecy of the triumph of the Immaculata:

> **We do not believe that that glorious day is far off, nor that it is simply a dream, when the statue of the Immaculata will be enthroned, thanks to her missionaries, in the very heart of Moscow.**
>
> **Maximilian Kolbe, Rome Conference, 11 February 1937**

When Fr. Maximilian-Mary Kolbe undertook a missionary journey to the Far East to make God known to the immensity of Asia through the mediation of the Immaculata, he was advised against this approach. He was advised that he should first teach about God and once having done this, then he should speak about the Mother of God. However, the name of Mary was always present both in his words and his writings, even when he was addressing the pagans. He believed that the Immaculata, being the distributor of all graces, would also grant the grace of conversion provided that one brought souls into contact with her in some way or another: either through her image or through words specifically addressed to her. He also wanted to show every missionary that the most effective missionary method involves acting through the intermediary of the Immaculata (*Life of Fr. Maximilian Kolbe,* Jerzy Domanski, Collectanea Theologica, Warsaw, 1971, p.27):

> **This interior life with the Immaculata, this harmonious fidelity in all things to the wishes and desires of his Mother and Queen, explains the success of his apostolic work.**
> **Fr. Gabriel Allegra, Director of Biblical Studies, Hong Kong, 1954**

In the 18th Century, St. Louis Mary de Montfort wrote *True Devotion to Mary.* It was mysteriously lost before ever making its appearance. It reappeared only in 1842. It was in this book that St. Louis wrote:

> **Great men are to come. But Mary is the one who shall fashion them by order of the Most High for the purpose of extending His empire over that of the godless, idolaters and Mohammedans. But when and how shall this come to pass? God alone knows. As for us, we have but to remain silent and pray, sigh and wait.**
> *True Devotion,* **Nos. 56-59**

St. Louis de Montfort develops the "affective" or human side of being devoted to Holy Mary. He explains that this discovery of Mary and progress in the understanding of her role is characteristic *of the latter times.*

The greatest saints, the souls richest in graces and virtues, shall be the most diligent in praying to our Blessed Lady, and in having her always present as their perfect model for imitation and their powerful aid.

I have said that this would come to pass particularly at the end of the world, and indeed, very soon, because the Most High with His Blessed Mother will form great saints unto Themselves...

Full of grace and zeal, these great souls shall be chosen to match themselves against God's enemies, who shall rage on all sides. And they shall be singularly devout to our Blessed Lady, illuminated by her light; strengthened with her nourishment; led by her spirit, supported by her arm and sheltered under her protection; so that they shall fight with one hand and build with the other.

It was through Mary that the salvation of the world was begun, and it is through Mary that it must be consummated...God wishes to reveal to us, Mary, the masterpiece of His hands, in the latter times.

True Devotion, No. 46-50

Vision of Holy Mary and Holy Mass

St. John Bosco was the founder the Salesian Order. On May 30, 1862, he had one of his most famous "dreams." It concerned the battle for the Church against many adversaries, the suffering Marian Pope, the glorious Marian Pope; and the final triumph, through devotion to the Holy Eucharist and Holy Mary.

His prophetic vision complements Fatima and is used to help ascertain and confirm the specific contents of the Third Revelation of Fatima. *(Forty Dreams of St. John Bosco,* TAN, Rockford, Il.) As at Fatima, St. John Bosco assures us that victory will be attained through Our Lady, who will win for her popes the graces to return to proper pope-ing.

> **Today, it is the Catholic Church herself that is under attack. In her functions, in her sacred institutions, in her Head, in her doctrine and in her discipline, she is assailed as Catholic Church, as center of the truth, as mistress of all the faithful.**
>
> **And it is to merit Heaven's special protection that we have recourse to Mary, as the Mother of us all, as the special help of Catholic kings and peoples, of Catholics all over the world.**
> **John Bosco, *Wonders of the Mother of God,* Turn, 1868, p. 7**

100

CHAPTER 13

MARY'S END-TIMES APOSTLES AND THE FATIMA MESSAGE

Mary's end-times apostles are characterized by deep devotion to Holy Mass and Holy Mary (as well as, deep and proper devotion to valid, properly functioning priests). Additionally, Mary's Remnant must cultivate devotion to the Two Hearts of Jesus and Mary.

St. Louis de Montfort explicitly declares that the heel of the Blessed Virgin is the Order of Mary's Apostles of the Latter Times. This heel will crush Satan's head:

> **It is true, great God: the devil will set great snares at the heel of this mysterious Woman, as You have foretold—that is, this little company of her children which will come at the end of the world—and there will be great enmities between this blessed posterity of Mary and the cursed race of Satan. But it is a wholly divine enmity, and the only one of which You are the author.**

But those combats and persecutions which the children of the race of Belial will wage against the race of your Blessed Mother will serve only to manifest the power of Your grace, the courage of their virtue and the authority of Your Mother.

Prophetic Prayer, St. Louis Mary de Montfort

Mary Protects Her Own

In Japan, Our Lady has already shown how she protects her Remnant. The Jesuits praying the Rosary in Hiroshima (when the bomb fell) were preserved from harm. Also, Kolbe's city of the Immaculata in Nagasaki was likewise spared annihilation from the bomb. The great saint of the Immaculata gave Mary's Remnant his last testament as follows:

My little children, love the Immaculata, love the Immaculata, love the Immaculata. She will make you happy. Trust her, turn yourselves over to her completely, without setting limits...It isn't given to everyone to understand the Immaculata but only to those who ask for this grace on their knees. The Immaculata is the Mother of God. Do you know what that means, 'Mother of God'? Truly, really *Mother of God!* Only the Holy Spirit can make His spouse known to whom and as He wills.

St. Maximilian Kolbe, *Soul Magazine,* July 1994

102

Devotion to the Immaculate Heart

To save the souls of poor sinners who are going to Hell, God wants to establish in the world devotion to my Immaculate Heart.
Our Lady of Fatima

What a moving revelation this is! God's merciful desire is to save the souls of poor sinners. He calls upon Mary's Remnant to contribute to this salvation by the means He has decreed in accordance with His Will, which is a grandiose flowering of universal devotion to the Immaculate Heart (and, thereby, devotion to Holy Mass).

Although declassified and vilified by Cardinal Ratzinger et al, as being merely an optional and irrelevant "private revelation," does not the Divine Will expressed by the Fatima Message and by other Marian messages bind the establishment church to be totally devoted to the Two Hearts and to restore proper devotion to Holy Mass and Holy Mary? The devotions of the Fatima children centered on pursuing the salvation of multitudes of poor sinners "destined for Hell" along with a special love of the Immaculate Heart of Mary, beyond doubt dearest to the Sacred Heart of Jesus.

While Francisco strived to be the consoler of the Holy Hearts of Jesus and Mary, Jacinta wanted to be their cooperatrix. Her dominant

thought... was for the salvation of souls...a missionary zeal for their conversion.

The Whole Truth About Fatima, Frere Michel, Vol. 2. Order: 1-800-263-8160

As a young postulant, Sister Lucy of Fatima, was visited by Our Lady and the Child Jesus. This is her account:

The Most Holy Virgin appeared...and by her side, elevated on a luminous cloud, was the Child Jesus. The Most Holy Virgin rested her hand on her shoulder, and as she did so, she showed her heart encircled by thorns, which she was holding in her other hand. At the same time, the Child said: 'Have compassion on the Heart of your Most Holy Mother, covered with thorns, with which ungrateful men pierce it at every moment, and there is no one to make an act of Reparation to remove them.' Then the Most Holy Virgin said: 'Look, my daughter, at my Heart, surrounded with thorns with which ungrateful men pierce me at every moment by their blasphemies and ingratitude. You, at least, try to console me and announce in my name that I promise to assist at the moment of death, with all the graces necessary for salvation, all those who, on the First Saturday of five consecutive months shall confess, receive Holy Communion, recite five decades of the Rosary and keep me company for fifteen minutes while meditating on the fifteen mysteries of the Rosary, with the intention of making Reparation to me.

Sister Lucy, Pontevedra, Spain, 1925, *Documentos,* p. 403

Again, Holy Mary and Holy Mass are united. One leads to the other. However, in the west, as the Canonized Latin Mass disappears, Mary's Remnant will lessen.

Must one look to Holy Russia to bring one into the Era of Fatima Blessings? Eventually, a large part of Mary's Remnant will be Holy Russia, the people whom God demands to be papally consecrated to the Immaculate Heart of Mary. Most likely, through the Canonized Eastern Rite Holy Mass, they will convert the world. Through Holy Russia, Holy Mass and Holy Mary will be restored to their proper places. Then Holy Church will once again prosper.

> **They overcame him [Satan] by the Blood of the Lamb [Holy Mass].**
> *Apoc 12:11*

CHAPTER 14

THE THIRD SECRET MUST CONERN THE GLORIOUS MARIAN POPE

In the end, my Immaculate Heart will triumph.
Our Lady of Fatima

The glorious Marian Pope will eagerly embrace and execute the God-given Fatima opportunity/command. He will bring about Holy Russia by consecrating Russia to the Immaculate Heart of Mary, in the way prescribed by Our Lady at Fatima.

A thought experiment helps one to understand and appreciate God's Fatima-given "consecration plan." Suppose your local priest or bishop loved you so much as to consecrate you to God. You would then be set aside (made a "holy other") to be made holy with or by (con–with; secrate–make holy) the one to whom you were consecrated (in order to bring yourself and others unto greater holiness). Holy Russia will come into being through its God-commanded consecration to Holy Mary.

Can a child be consecrated to God by his father? Can a God-given authority over an individual consecrate that individual to God? For example, can the head of a household consecrate his family to God? Of course.

Ever more so, the Holy Father is *the Father.* He is the God-designated Vicar of men to God. He is the new Adam on earth. In his office, he is also Vicar of Christ. As such, in a uniquely superior way, he can consecrate individuals to God. In doing so, he honors them by setting them aside as special agents for God.

The power of consecrating a people to the Immaculata has been proven. For example, although being a "shadow of Russian consecration," the proper consecration of Portugal bestowed upon it God's special blessings: *"In Portugal, the dogma of the faith will always be maintained."*

Why will it be maintained in Portugal? It will be maintained because this land was consecrated to the Immaculate Heart of Mary by its bishops, in full agreement with its civil authorities and people.

A specifically Fatima-commanded, official and full papal consecration, along with all of his subservient bishops, is the consecration demanded by God to bring mankind into the era of Fatima Blessings. The Holy Father, as Vicar of Christ on earth, can consecrate any individual or group of individuals. Certainly, in the name of God, and by God's command, he can and should consecrate Russia to the Immaculata. By his properly executed Fatima-commanded consecration of Russia, the glorious Marian Pope will "activate Fatima Blessings" upon Russia and the world.

One should appreciate and regard positively what Our Lady has requested in order to activate the Fatima Blessings upon the Russian people, the Church, the rest of the world and individuals (now and eternally). God Himself has ordered the Pope and his bishops to bless in a very special way "His Russia;" or, from the western point of view, to bless Holy Russia into being.

The glorious Marian Pope will consecrate (set aside in the name of God) the Russian people to the special patronage and service of the Immaculata, to be under her special protection and favor. This is an awesome privilege and blessing for the Russian people. They are to be dedicated to the Immaculata. They are to be Holy Russia. They are to be converted and to convert the world.

Once again, as with Abraham (the father of the Jewish people and our father in the Catholic Faith) and the Hebrew people, "the initiative of grace and mercy" was made by God, not men. The Russian people haven't taken the initiative. They didn't ask for such a consecration. Perhaps, because of their outstanding devotion to Theotokos, the ever Immaculate Mother of God, they have been granted this honor by Holy Mary. No other nation on earth has ever been chosen by name by Our Lady for her work in such an explicit way. (It is no wonder that evil powers within Russia, united with evil dysfunctional upper clergymen, devised and continue to implement the Vatican-Moscow Concordat and its demonic spirit.)

According to the Fatima Message, that awesome day of Marian Consecration by the Marian Pope, together with all of his subservient bishops, will also be a day of vowed reparation to the Immaculate Heart of Mary: which vowed reparation (as this book has demonstrated) must be liturgical reparation–the reinstatement (or restoration to par) of the Canonized Mass Latin Liturgy.

The glorious Marian Pope will abandon wicked, man-made geopolitical schemes. Trusting God, he will eagerly embrace and execute the God-given Fatima opportunity. Thereby, he will bring upon the whole world an era of Fatima Blessings.

Deo gratias. Maria gratias.

CHAPTER 15

CRUCIAL POPES OF MODERN TIMES

Heaven's apocalyptic Fatima Message prophetically assures us that it is all up to the Pope. He alone is Vicar of mankind to God. He alone is the present-day Adam. He can act like a devil and be condemned by Christ for so doing. He can be like unto the first Peter, whom Christ condemned as "devil" (Mt 16:25).

Or, the Pope can function as God's instrument, as His prophetic Fatima Message exhorts: to bring Holy Church, Holy Mass, Holy Mary and Holy Russia back among us. Only then will we enjoy an era of Fatima Blessings. To repeat, it is all up to the Marian Pope. It is all up to us, by our prayers and sacrifices, to bring about the Marian Pope.

In 1903, Pope (Saint)Pius X echoed a Fatima principle: "It is all up to the Pope," while disclosing the heart of the problem which has led Our Lady (of modern times) to come to us as Our Lady of the Canonized Mass:

We understand that it belonged to Us, in virtue of the pontifical office entrusted to Us, to provide a remedy for such a great evil [apostasy from God]. We believed that this order of God was addressed to Us: 'Behold, today I set you over nations and kingdoms, to tear down and destroy, to build up and to plant' (Jer 1,10)...It is necessary, by every means, and at the price of any effort, to uproot entirely *this monstrous and detestable iniquity proper to the times we are living in, and through which man substitutes himself for God...*We must necessarily and firmly fear whether such a perversion of minds is not the sign announcing, and the beginning of the last times, and that the Son of Perdition spoken of by the Apostle (11Thess 2,3) might already be living on this earth...[Man even strives to] dedicate the visible world to himself in the guise of the temple, where he pretends to receive the adoration of his own kind... *"He sits in the temple of God, and gives himself out as if he were God"* (11Thess 2,4).
Pope St. Pius X, *E Supremi Apostolatus Cathedra (From My Supreme Apostolic Throne)*

In his dogmatic encyclical, Pope St. Pius X recognizes "that it is all up to the Pope." The Pope alone is Vicar of mankind to God, as well as, Vicar of Christ to mankind. The reigning pope acts and speaks as he should, or refuses to do so. God, through His Mother, Mary, has "raised the stakes." The Pope either embraces the Fatima Opportunity/Command or suffers the consequences.

Great Pre-1929 Modern Popes

In God's Providence, the modern popes preceding 1929 led themselves and their flocks to yearn for or devoutly anticipate the God-given Fatima Message and, thus, to set up an atmosphere which would profit from its coming. Pope Saint Pius V (1566-1572), responding to the directives of the Council of Trent, saw the horror of those who attempted to destroy the Holy Sacrifice of the Mass and issued *Quo Primum,* thus canonizing in perpetuity, the form (exact words) of the Holy Sacrifice of the Mass for the Latin Rite. In doing so, he canonized the God-given way to properly and fully honor Holy Mary.

Pope Gregory XVI (1831-1846) condemned liberalism which was rampant in the Church (in his encyclical, *Mirari vos,* 1832). This liberalism was destined eventually to flower into apostasy within. He also promoted the dogma of the Immaculate Conception of the Blessed Virgin Mary without defining it as a dogma of faith.

Pope Pius IX (1846-1878), although his papacy was fraught with difficulties, such as the voluntary imprisonment of the popes in the Vatican (until 1929), defined as dogma, the Immaculate Conception of the

Blessed Virgin Mary (1854). In his encyclical, *Quanta Cura* (1869), accompanied by the famous *Syllabus,* he reiterated the condemnation of pantheism, naturalism, socialism, communism, freemasonry and other doctrinal errors of religious liberalism. He condemned the sources of our present Novus Ordo Religion, the anti-Mary and anti-Holy Mass ecclesial power.

In order to distinguish among the various functions of the Bishop of Rome (acting as bishop, as Patriarch, as universal Pope non-bindingly, or as universal Pope bindingly) this Pope also summoned the Vatican Council One. He promulgated its decree, *Pastor Aeternus* (1870), which defined the nature of the dogma of papal infallibility in simple terms.

Providentially, his dogmatic pronouncement would help the faithful to reject the Bishop of Rome's sinful actions and non-dogmatic decrees. Thus, Holy Mass and Holy Mary could be protected against papal assault.

It was Pope Leo XIII(1878-1903)who added/commanded the Leonine Prayers after Mass, especially, the Prayer to the Archangel Michael, which included prophetic warnings regarding the church and the papacy. In his unabridged Leonine Prayer, he stated that the Chair of

Peter would become the souce of "abominable impiety."

Pope Saint Pius X (1903-1914) published the decree, *Lamentabili Sani* (1907) condemning the works of Modernist writers and issued the encyclical, *Pascendi,* in which he outlined the errors of Modernism, described as "the synthesis of all heresies." He suppressed modernist teachers and, in 1910, required priests to take the Anti-Modernist oath.

Pope Benedict XV (1914-1922) promulgated the Code of Canon Law in 1917. His reign was an overture to the reigns of his two successors. Much that they achieved was initiated by him. The initial Fatima Message (1917) constituted an immediate answer to Pope Benedict's (1917) plea for guidance and a solution for the "ecclesial apocalyptic problem." However, Our Lady's command for the papal/ episcopal Consecration of Russia did not come until six years after his death.

CHAPTER 16

THE CRITICAL POST-1929 POPES

The year, 1929, is the year Sr. Lucy experienced the Salutary Theophany of the Canonized Mass. Also, at this vision, the Fatima command to consecrate Russia was given. This year constitutes the dividing line between pre-1929 and post-1929 events. Pope Pius XI (1922-1939) reigned during this time.

In the case of Pius XI, as well as, Pope Pius XII and also the Vatican Two popes, one cannot make an absolute judgment, merely a rational operative conclusion or conjecture. More precisely, none will ever know whether these popes were forcefully or skillfully manipulated, cleverly duped, or lied to by the evil experts (perceived and condemned by Pope St. Pius X). One will never know whether internal upper level politics (such as that exemplified by Cardinals Casaroli and Sodano) pushed the Pope into inculpable behavior; or, if such politics prevailed over the Pope's will. However, "phenomenologically, or from a positivist or operational viewpoint," Pope Pius XI, Pope Pius XII and all the Vatican Two popes (from Pope John XXIII into the present, except Pope John Paul I) rejected the Fatima Message (although, at times, in a neo-Hegelian way).

Keeping in mind previous remarks, it would seem that Pope Pius XI (the first pope commanded by Fatima to make the proper Fatima consecration/reparation) failed to obey at the time he became aware of them because a solemn act of consecration of Russia (by the Pope and all the bishops of the world) would have implied a formal, doctrinal condemnation of Marxism-Leninism and a resolute policy to oppose Bolshevik Russia. Politically, the papal territory had just obtained national status by the Lateran Treaty (1929). Why should Pope Pius XI jeopardize this newly secured, still unstable victory?

His successor, Pope Pius XII, apparently also opted for the "politically safe" alternative. During these post-1929 pontificates, the Holy See embarked on a path of compromise, even complicity. As persecution in Russia was becoming increasingly more brutal, Pope/Rome was seeking a *modus vivendi* with the Soviets and was operating merely a make-believe apostolate in Soviet Russia.[1] (*Fatima, joie intime,* p. 209-210)

---

[1]

A similar propagandized "must-believe; make-believe" message that Russia has been converted characterizes the papal reign of John Paul II.

Popes React to History

Pope Pius XII died on 9 October 1958, and was succeeded by Pope John XXIII. In February 1960, a Vatican press release made it known that the Third Secret would not be revealed. Lucy was, indeed, a prophet when she said to Father Fuentes:

> **Father, we should not wait for an appeal to come from Rome, on behalf of the Holy Father, calling on the whole world to do penance. Nor should we wait for it to come from our bishops in their dioceses or from the religious congregations. No. Our Lord has already made frequent use of these means and the world took no notice. That is why each of us must now begin his own spiritual reform. Each person must not only save his own soul, but also all the souls that God has placed on his path.**
> **Sister Lucy, Conversation with Fr. Fuentes, 1957**

The politically expedient policy of some "post-1929 popes" to "open to the East" was the major obstacle to the accomplishment of God's great design revealed at Tuy for the conversion of Russia and the peace of the world. Once informed of the request for the consecration of Russia (in 1930-31) Pope Pius XI maintained an icy silence about Fatima, clearly refusing to be perceived as having a nun dictate to him a policy and an action that

119

went against his own geopolitically correct plans (even if such advice were for the good of the Church and the peace of the world).*(Fatime, joie intime, p. 212)*

Many are shocked that most of the post-1929 popes preferred man to God; human solutions to the divine solution; and that they lacked trust in God: that God knows what is best. Is Sister Lucy correct in stating that they are victims of "diabolic delusions?"

Lastly, the faithful marvel that "consecrating Russia to the Immaculate Heart of Mary" could ever be taken as an insult to Russia. Were popes from 1929 onward faithless? At least, were they lacking in faith when they refused to abandon natural expediency in order to embrace God-given opportunity?

After the Tuy-1929 command/opportunity was papally rejected, Sister Lucy received the complaints of Our Lord, in Rianjo, near Pontevedra, where she had been sent to rest:

> **Make it know to My ministers that, given that they are imitating the King of France in delaying the execution of My request, so they will follow him into misfortune. However, it will never by too late to have recourse to Jesus and to Mary.**
>
> *Fatime, joie intime, p. 213*

In 1929-31, as subsequently even into our times, everything depends on the Pope. If Russia had been consecrated to the Immaculate Heart of Mary, Russia would have been converted; and neither the Second World War, nor the lightning expansion of Communism, (its main beneficiary) would have taken place.

One sadly recalls Our Lady's prediction that this horrible war would begin in the reign of Pius XI. This war (World War II) and its consequences could have been prevented had this Pope opted for obedience to God over politics to men.[1]

At the beginning of 1944, Sister Lucy expressed her desire to speak personally to Pope Pius XII. She had just committed the Third Secret to writing. But 1944 was the year in which Fr. Dhanis began his offensive against Fatima–which offensive climaxed in Rome's Millennial Fatima Message (2000).

Fr. Dhanis reduced the Fatima Message to a believable generic call to penance, outright rejecting the particular defining elements within it. In effect, he likened Sr. Lucy's Fatima Message to the "pietistic ravings" of an overly zealous nun. This tactic was so successful that

---

[1] See *The Whole Truth About Fatima,* Vol. 2, pp 695-700 for proof that World War II began when God predicted it would begin.

Pope Pius XII would not even receive Sister Lucy.

In August 1959 (according to Cardinal Ottaviani and Msgr. Loris Capovilla, a papal advisor and secretary) *"The secret was delivered to the new Pope, John XXIII, still sealed."* (It is interesting to note that, Malachi Martin, who read it, said the Third Secret was addressed to the Pope of 1960.) When he read it, Pope John XXIII made no official public statement concerning the secret. In his decision not to reveal the Secret in 1960, Pope John XXIII showed his disdain towards Fatima.

> **He stated the text did not pertain to his times and that he preferred to leave an assessment of its text to his successors.**
> Fr. Alonso, quote, concerning *Pope John XXIII's private statement* after reading the Third Secret.

In 1963, Pope Paul VI succeeded Pope John XXIII. It is reported that his reading of the Third Secret influenced his homily for the 50th Fatima Anniversary in 1967:

> **The first intention is for the Church: the Church, One, Holy, Catholic and Apostolic. We want to pray, as we have said, for its internal peace. What terrible damage could be provoked by arbitrary interpretations, not authorized by the teaching of the Church, disrupting its traditional and constitutional structure, replacing the theology of the true and great**

Fathers of the Church with new and peculiar ideologies; interpretations intent upon stripping the norms of faith of that which modern thought, often lacking rational judgment, does not understand and does not like...We want to ask of Mary , a living Church, a true Church, a united Church, a holy Church.

Pope Paul VI, *remarks, 50ᵗʰ Anniversary Fatima, 1967*

Characteristically, the enigmatic Pope Paul VI managed to underline Fatima while rejecting it. Upon his return from Fatima, he had a conversation with Jean Guitton, his close friend and confidante:

What impression did Lucy make on you?

–Oh! replied the Pope. She is an uncomplicated peasant woman. The people wanted to see her, so I showed her to them.

Pope Paul VI, conversation reported by and with Jean Guitton

Would John Paul I have been the Marian Pope, had he lived? He had visited with Sr. Lucy in 1977. During his brief pontificate, he is reported to have stated:

If I live [long enough] he declared to those close to him, I shall return to Fatima to consecrate the people of Russia to the Blessed Virgin, in accordance with the instructions she has given to Sr. Lucy.

John Paul I and Fatima, Catholic Counter Revolution, No. 288, Sept. 1996, p.12

Pope John Paul II read the secret along with the Prefect for the Congregation for the Doctrine of the Faith, Joseph Cardinal Ratzinger. Why did this Pope/Rome (and the previous ones) prefer geopolitical strategy or expedience to religious obedience to God? Why does the establishment church (since 1960) not only disobey God, but also justify this disobedience with cover-ups? Is the Vatican-Moscow Concordat the reason?

Vatican-Moscow Agreement

The Vatican-Moscow Agreement of 1962 is a matter of historical record. Pope John XXIII conceded to the Soviet negotiator Msgr. Nikodim, a KGB agent, the promise not to censure Communism or the Soviet regime. In exchange, Russian Orthodox observers (quite likely, KGB agents) would be permitted to attend the Second Vatican Council. Cardinal Tisserant conducted these negotiations with Nikodim at Metz, France in 1962. Tisserant may have simply been following orders from Pope John or his "shadow" Cardinal Montini [the future Pope Paul VI].

However, these negotiations represented a break with the traditional teaching of the Church, in particular, Pope

Pius XI's *Divini Redemptoris*. This break guaranteed repercussions for the Fatima Message and those trying to propagate it. Because Pope John XXIII feared Russia, he wanted schismatic Russian Orthodox bishops present at the council, even though it would be at a high price. He accepted peace "at Russia's price."[1]

Pope John XXIII pursued this course of action in spite of his awareness that the Third Secret insisted that the Pope consecrate Russia to the Immaculate Heart of Mary along with the Catholic Bishops of the world. Otherwise, nations would lose the faith and the clergy would fall into Hell like leaves falling from a tree in autumn.

Pope John XXIII seemed to have (wrongly) perceived the Marian Consecration in a negative manner. He (and his advisors) saw the Fatima Consecration as labeling Russia as evil and sinful. He feared that Kruschev might take such an act as an insult or even respond with a declaration of war.

It appears that Pope John XXIII loved and feared man more than God. In effect, the "steering powers of Vatican Two" sold out Mary for Moscow, in exchange for worldly peace and ecumenical unity. By consenting to

---

[1] **The result of this agreement was that Communism could not be condemned at Vatican Two.**

and implementing the Vatican-Moscow Concordat, the powers of Vatican Two trampled on Fatima, disobeyed God and insulted the Blessed Virgin Mary.[1]

Now one can begin to understand why the Second Vatican Council glaringly failed to issue a condemnation of the worst enemy of God in our day– communism, or, in Our Lady's terms–Russia's Errors. It would prove helpful at this point to carefully read *Gaudium et Spes* (77-93); Pope Paul VI's United Nations' speech; and the Novus Ordo Mass, with the Vatican-Moscow Concordat in mind.

---

[1]
In fairness to Pope John XXIII, John Cardinal Heenan assured us that the Pope regretted starting Vatican II shortly after it began. Also, Jean Guitton informs us that this Pope's last words were: *"Stop the Council!"* See www.traditio.com for more information.

CHAPTER 17

NO FATIMA CONSECRATION
NO RUSSIAN CONVERSION

Pope/Rome's preferential love of (naturally sinful) Russia, man and the New Age was hidden from public view by a series of mock consecrations, followed by clumsily engineered Fatima cover-ups. Such consecrations and cover-ups can be outlined as follows:

1) The Consecration of Russia to the Immaculate Heart of Mary–by the Pope in union with the Catholic bishops of the world–was demanded by God through Our Lady of Fatima in 1929 at Tuy. Our Lady said:

> **The moment has come in which God asks of the Holy Father to make, and to order that in union with him and at the same time, all the bishops of the world make the consecration of Russia to My Immaculate Heart, promising to convert it because of this day of prayer and world-wide reparation.**
>
> *The Whole Truth About Fatima*, Frere Michel de la Sainte Trinite, 1-800-263-8160

2) Between 1929 and 1984, consecrations were done–yet none of them complied with God's demands. Therefore, World War II happened and subsequently, Russia's Errors spread throughout the world, along with wars, persecutions and much suffering.

3) In Rome, on March 25, 1984, the Pope after sending an invitation (and not a papal command) to the bishops to join him–consecrated the world, not Russia, to the Immaculate Heart of Mary. This consecration was "of the world and not of Russia;" and was not done with all of the Pope's bishops. In fact, Sister Lucy testified that *"Many bishops did not attach any importance to it."*

In fact, at the Vatican, on March 25, 1984, (Pope John Paul II consecrated the *world,* soon to be propagandized as being the day of the Consecration of Russia). By his own words, the Pope himself admitted that Russia was not consecrated:

> **Enlighten, especially, the peoples whose consecration and entrustment [by us to] You are awaiting.**
> **John Paul II, L'Osservatore Romano, 3/26/84, pp. 1-6**

What changed Pope/Rome's speech (not "mind")? Perestroika and Glasnost (the sixth in Russia's history) were declared in 1989. Gorbachev was proclaimed the Global Master and given Time's 1990 Man of the Year

Award, together with the Nobel Peace Prize for 1990. *The man who caused the Gulf Crisis of 1990 was given the Peace Prize!*

The Vatican-Moscow agreement or "marriage" produced its first "child"–Glasnost (1989). With this "child," the promise of New Order Salvation is given.

Glasnost's "Vatican parent" (in 1989 and thereafter) assumed that the precious child, "Glasnost," must have been conceived on March 25, 1984. In 1989, both parents celebrated Glasnost's birthday in Rome:

> **On December 1, 1989, Gorbachev met with Pope John Paul II and promised religious freedom. The Holy Father referred to this meeting as a "sign of the times...a sign that is rich in promise." The Pope would say that this meeting was "Divine Providence."**
> *Soul Magazine*, **January-February 2001**

Also, on this occasion, Pope John Paul II regularized the Rome/Moscow fruitful marriage. He gave it somewhat of a *"sanatio in radice"* by formally pronouncing Gorbachev (the dedicated and unrepentant militant atheist), to be a "crypto-Christian" (a Christian, no matter what contrary evidence existed).

The mega-power in the Church decreed a new formula

for unity and faithfulness. One must believe the party-line: Russia was consecrated as Fatima requested in 1984. Rome and Moscow were united in blissful union.

The media imaged a "new or inconsistent" Sister Lucy. Aided by cardinals and bishops, Father Robert Fox and a few "experts," the new party line was presented. The new party-line was New Age Unity, Peace and Safety, as we follow the Red Dragon into a heaven on earth. However, it should be crystal clear by now, that, in order to follow the Dragon, one must abandon Our Lady.

No Consecration Therefore No Conversion
No Conversion Therefore No Consecration

If Russia had been consecrated as God demanded at Fatima, it would have been converted by now. However, Russia has not been converted. Therefore, all of the alleged valid consecrations, especially that of 1984, are to be considered invalid and not done as God requires. The establishment is mistaken or has deliberately lied or covered up the embarrassing truth.

Since the alleged consecration of Russia in 1984, Russia has undergone a spiritual, moral and

material collapse. Even the Russian Orthodox Patriarch, Alexy II, has decried the spiritual decomposition of Russian society since 'the fall of communism.'...Russia has not even converted to the Orthodox religion: 94% of Russians aged 19-29 do not go to church...the total number of Russian Catholics is 110,000–in a nation of 145 million people...less than 1/10 of one percent of the population. In all of Russia, there is a grand total of 114 priests, only three of whom were trained and ordained in Russia.

There are now two abortions for every live birth in Russia...The situation is so desperate that Russian nationalist Vladimir Zhirinovsky is advocating polygamy to produce more babies....

The liberal journalist David Frum, writing in *The National Post,* declares, "In Russia, Putin's in–and democracy is out." His article details Vladimir Putin's systematic "reconstruction of an authoritarian state in Russia controlled by more or less the same people who controlled the Soviet state that collapsed in 1991."
Christopher Ferrara, Esq., "When Black Is White," *Fatima Crusader,* Winter 2001, p.11

Obviously, the act of 25 March 1984, in no way corresponded to Our Lady's request since it has not produced Russia's conversion. By 1992, in the spatially enormous (strictly) Russian nation of which Mgr.

Kondrusiewicz is apostolic administrator, there are actually only six priests serving six very small "churchless" parishes (Abbe de Nantes, C.C.R. Jan. 1992, p.8).

Russia has forbidden even the possibility of its conversion. In March 2001, the Russian Duma took official action to forbid the growth of Catholicism in Russia (*National Catholic Register*, March 2001). Unbelievably, the same Pope/Rome establishment (which demands belief in Russia's consecration) has agreed to the possibility of its not being converted:

> **The Russian Orthodox Church argues vigorously that nearly all of the former Soviet Union constitutes its "canonical territory" and is off limits to Catholic evangelization. To date, the Vatican seems to have tacitly respected this claim.**
> *Our Sunday Visitor*, **editorial, Apr. 15, 2001, "No Welcome Mat for Pope"**

Incredibly, while agreeing with the party lie concerning Russia's conversion, Archbishop Tadeusz Kondrusiewicz made an official apology for being so Catholic as to wish to convert Russians to Catholicism. How can anyone believe in Rome's Millennial Fatima Message when even the spokes-clergyman for the Russian Catholic hierarchy denies its bold claim that Russia has already been converted:

In his 2001 *ad limina* visit to the Pope, Archbishop Kondrusiewicz, speaking for the Russian Catholic hierarchy, asked "pardon for our errors," and issued an invitation for the Pontiff to visit Russia. The primary focus of his remarks, however, was the effort to promote better relations with the Russian Orhodox Church. Despite the efforts of the Catholic hierarchy,the Archbishop lamented, ecumenical progress is hampered by "the continual, unjustified accusations, on the part of the Russian Orthodox Church, of proselytism and penetration of their 'canonical territory.'" The Orthodox Church has consistently argued that Catholics should not attempt to win converts in a land that is historically affiliated with the Orthodox faith–even if the practice of that faith has waned.

The Catholic World Report, March 2001, p.16

Can one believe Pope/Rome's propaganda? Can one believe lies such as these: (that) conversion is any type of good change of heart; the world is Russia; a non-collegial consecration is a collegial consecration; the existential church has been "repared;" peace prevails throughout the world; and, Russia, having been converted, now evangelizes the rest of the world, bringing it into authentic Catholicism?

The Abomination of Desolation

This abomination of desolation is spiritual. Specifically, it is liturgical (Mt 24:15). Hence, the appropriate liturgy for the New World Order is the Novus Ordo Liturgy.

During the "abomination of desolation," the good will perceive the truth and react accordingly. On the other hand, evil people will rejoice in the darkness.

> **According to Augustine, towards the end of the world, there will be a general persecution of the good by the wicked: so that at the same time, some will fear, namely the good, and some will be secure, namely the wicked. The words: 'When they shall say: Peace and Security' refer to the wicked; who will pay little heed to the signs of the coming judgment; while the words of Luke XXI.26, 'men withering away,' etc. should be referred to the good.**
> **St. Thomas Acquinas**

The faithful are persecuted and are martyred–not only by the anti-God factions of the world; but also, by fallen away Catholics, such as Novus Ordo popes, along with many cardinals, bishops, priests, etc., who, not only remain within the establishment church, but also dictatorially govern this church in an "apocalyptically Beastly" manner. Ideologies clash and the anti-God factions are prevailing. The good suffer. The evil rejoice.

Eventually, the piper will be paid. God's wrath will destroy Satan's New Order. The Fatima Message assures that the imposition of an "anti-Catholic" or "anti-God" order brings with it the destruction of God's economy and thus, famines, false peace, demonic deception, wars and the annihilation of nations.

Today, Satan has seated himself within the sanctuary of the Catholic Church, (as Pope Leo XIII fearfully predicted; and, as Pope Paul VI clearly confirmed); and is bringing about the abomination of desolation.

However, Mary's Remnant can be consoled. The Marian Pope will come. He will accomplish the Fatima Consecration. Our Lady of Fatima assures us "it will be" even though "it will be late:"

> **In the end, my Immaculate Heart will triumph, the Holy Father will consecrate Russia to me, Russia will be converted and a period of peace will be granted to mankind.**
> **Our Lady of Fatima, last sentence of the Third Revelation**

CHAPTER 18

POPE/ROME'S MILLENNIAL FATIMA MESSAGE

In the morning of May 13, 2000, Pope John Paul II beatified Jacinta and Francisco of Fatima. After this Mass, Cardinal Sodano presented a preview of the Third Secret of Fatima, with his own brief exegesis.

On June 26, 2000, the Congregation of the Doctrine of the Faith, under Cardinal Ratzinger and Archbishop Bertone, released *"The Fatima Message."* This official publication, and all other millennial Fatima-originated propaganda emanating from Pope/Rome in 2000, is herein referred to as "Pope/Rome's Millennial Fatima Message," in contrast to Our Lady's Fatima Message.

"The Secret"
(According to Rome's Millennial Propaganda)

January 3, 1944

I write in obedience to you, My God, who command me to do so through His Excellency the bishop of Leira and through your Most Holy Mother and mine.

After the two parts which I have already explained, at the left of Our Lady and a little above, we saw an angel with a flaming sword in his left hand; flashing, it gave out flames that looked as though they would set the world on fire; but they died out in contact with the splendor that Our Lady radiated toward him from her right hand; pointing to the earth with his right hand, the angel cried out in a loud voice: 'Penance, Penance, Penance!'

And we saw in an immense light that is God: 'something similar to how people appear in a mirror when they pass in front of it'–a bishop dressed in white; 'we had the impression that it was the Holy Father.' Other bishops, priests, men and women religious going up a steep mountain, at the top of which there was a big cross of rough-hewn trunks as of a cork tree with the bark.

Before reaching there, the Holy Father passed through a big city half in ruins and half trembling with the halting steps, afflicted with pain and sorrow, he prayed for the souls of the corpses he met on his way; having reached the top of the mountain, on his knees at the foot of the big cross he was killed by a group of soldiers who fired bullets and arrows at him, and in the same way there died one after another the other bishops, priests men and women religious, and various lay people of different ranks and positions.

Beneath the two arms of the cross there were two angels each with a crystal aspersorium in his hand, in which they gathered up the blood of the martyrs and with it sprinkled the souls that were making their way to God.

Lucia dos Santos

Evaluating Pope/Rome's "Third Secret" Text

In order to ascertain the veracity of any claim to authenticity for an alleged "Third Secret," certain positive generic criteria must be established and subsequently be validated. These criteria have been established and have already been presented. To be authentic, the proposed Third Revelation of Fatima must indirectly or directly, presume, address, imply or concern: 1) fiducial apostasy; 2) liturgical apostasy; 3) God's wrath; 4) Mary's Remnant; and 5) the Marian Popes.

Rome's alleged "Third Secret" does not meet with the basic criteria (of Fatima knowledge and reality). It is glaringly in opposition to or even in contradiction to established facts (reality). Therefore, its claim to authenticity must be rejected.

Also, it is helpful to observe that if one wishes to establish the credibility of Pope/Rome's Millennial Third Secret, one needs to go beyond its conformity to one or two (but not all) positive traits. For example, a white male with black hair and a limp commits a crime. When one finds such a male, he hasn't necessarily found the perpetrator. Often, negative tests must be employed to rule out the suspect or to make a solid case against him. If one fact does not fit, "you must acquit." If one fact does not fit, one must reject even the possibility that Pope/Rome's proposed Millennial Third Secret is real, no matter who insists that it is.

Pope/Rome's alleged Third Secret does not fulfill previously established generic traits. It does not emphasize nor presume apostasy within and God's wrath; nor, does it address the glorious Marian Pope and the subsequent era of Fatima Blessings. Even more clearly, Pope/Rome's alleged Third Secret does not conform to what is certain and common knowledge of the first and last sentences of the Third Revelation of Fatima.

The Third Revelation definitely begins: *"In Portugal, the dogma* [not necessarily, the liturgy] *of the Faith will be retained..."* The God-given last sentence reads as follows: *"In the end, my Immaculate Heart will triumph, the Holy Father* [the second Marian Pope] *will consecrate* [set aside and dedicate] *Russia to me, Russia will be converted and a period of peace will be granted to mankind."*

Pope/Rome's proposed Third Secret text contradicts these known facts. It does not contain either sentence. It lacks two essential *"sine qua non"* traits demanded by God-given history–by the reality of what was previously disclosed by Sister Lucy as constituting the first and last sentences of the Third Secret.

An Evaluation

When one applies supportive and negating factors to

Pope/Rome's alleged Third Secret, one is forced to reject its claim to being the Third Secret text. However, it could constitute the description of a partial (not complete in itself) preparatory vision to the Third Revelation of Fatima. Only when taken as such can one contend that it is "part" of the Third Secret. Since there were preliminary visions for the First and Second Revelations, (the children saw Hell) a preliminary vision to the Third Revelation is credible. The following remarks of Blessed Jacinta to Lucia illustrate such a possibility:

> **All three of them had prostrated themselves on the ground and were reciting the prayers the Angel had taught them. Suddenly, Jacinta stood up and exclaimed: 'Oh, Lucy! Can't you see all those roads, all those paths and fields full of dead and bleeding people, and others who are crying with hunger and have nothing to eat? And the Holy Father in a church, praying before the Immaculate Heart of Mary? And people praying with him?'**
>
> **Several days later, she asked Lucy: 'Can I say that I saw the Holy Father and all those people?**
>
> **No! Her cousin answered sharply. Don't you see that that's part of the Secret? And that, if you do, the whole thing will soon be out?**
>
> **All right. Then I'll say nothing at all.'**
> *Francisco et Jacinta*, **p. 167**

Certain facts give credence to the possibility that Pope/Rome's alleged "Third Secret text" may really be a description of a preliminary or basic vision from which the actual Third Secret develops. For example, *"climbing a steep mountain"* describes a trip to Fatima (as well as, a difficult spiritual journey to God). The *"cork tree"* is a symbol of Portugal, as the maple tree symbolizes Canada. The cross could be fit into previous God-given symbolism as representing the Holy Sacrifice at the Canonized Mass.

Is this the Marian Pope who seeks to reestablish the Canonized Mass Liturgy? Is this the suffering Marian Pope destined for true martyrdom? Are these his subservient bishops struggling to "implement Fatima" and to reinstate the Canonized Mass Liturgy?

The answers to these questions are "no." Therefore, the possibility exists that this Pope/Rome "Third Secret text" describes a visionary basis for Our Lady's Third Secret. Obviously, *it is not Our Lady's of Fatima's Third Secret* as alleged by Pope/Rome in 2000.

Rome's Eye Witness

Many still have a blinding obedience to and trust in propaganda emanating from Pope/Rome. Such a "1984 mind-set" (to be taken as referring both to the famous novel, *1984* and to acceptance of the validity of the 1984 "consecration") leads them to readily and wholeheartedly accept Pope/Rome's alleged "confirmation of authenticity by Sister Lucy." After all, have they not been assured by Pope/Rome that Sister Lucy endorses and attests to the truth of Pope/Rome's Millennial Fatima Message?

However, one might ask such "blind followers of blind leaders" [Sister Lucy's words] to consider the following. Why didn't the only authentic living Fatima witness (who was physically present on May 13, 2000) attest to the authenticity of both Pope/Rome's Third Secret and to the 1984 "consecration?"

At least, why didn't Msgr. Bertone or Cardinal Sodano (Vatican Secretary of State), Cardinal Ratzinger or any other Vatican representative ask Sister Lucy legally or publicly to attest to the authenticity of the Third Secret as read aloud before her and others? Is it not odd that, (even though the only live witness is available and able to testify as to the validity of the 1984 consecration and to the authenticity of Rome's obviously fraudulent Third Secret) Sr. Lucy was permitted to attest only "by previous deposition to the contents of an envelope" as being "her letter;" and by a questionable eleven year old computer generated communique attesting to the veracity of these Rome-generated documents or deeds?

Is it not strange that Sister Lucy (who was physically present "to" Cardinal Sodano's millennial presentation of Pope/Rome's alleged Third Secret) was not permitted to confirm its authenticity? Instead, it is reported by a Blue Army member who was present there, that Sister Lucy flailed her arms in the air several times during the talk, during which she was surrounded by two bodyguards. Does not such behavior characterize a protestor or a drugged person?

Who Is Credible? What Is Credible?

Cardinal Ratzinger contended that one is free *not to believe in the Fatima Message;* however, one is not free to reject the Third Secret and its "past tense" application to Pope John Paul II (Cardinal Ratzinger, press conference, June, 2000). Pope/Rome demands assent (as to objective facts) for its claim that Pope John Paul II is the great Marian Pope of "their" alleged Third Secret. *"It lies in the facts, "*

145

contended Cardinal Ratzinger, as shown in the following interview:

> **To the journalist who asked him whether the message of Fatima represents a dogma of faith, the Cardinal answered:** *'No, not at all. There is no question of dogmas of faith when it comes to apparitions.'*
>
> **'So, one can refuse to believe in what happened at Fatima or Lourdes?' continued the journalist.**
>
> **'Of course,' answered the Cardinal.** *'One can also refuse to believe in the apparitions. I repeat, we are not in the presence of dogmas of faith.'*
>
> **'So, can we also refuse to believe in the connection between the Third Secret of Fatima and the attack against Pope Wojtyla on 13 May of 1981?' the journalist continued ironically.**
>
> *'The connection between the attack and the Third Secret is obvious. It lies in the facts.'* **answered Cardinal Ratzinger in a tone which brooked no reply...The press was awash with commentaries.**
> **Catholic Counter-Revolution, June 2000, p.13**

Pope/Rome expects blind obedience to its millennial interpretation of its alleged Third Secret. Yet, one is free to reject God and His Fatima Message.

Must one believe in the name of the "living magisterium" that the Fatima Message is "fulfilled and to be forgotten?" As an exercise of the allegedly "living magisterium," Archbishop Bertone (June 26, 2000) officially claimed that the 1984 Consecration of the World was, indeed, the Consecration of Russia. In doing so, he confirms the heinous purpose of Rome's Millennial Fatima Message: to bury the Fatima Message; to decree it as being "past and over with."

Furthermore, the astute observer will notice that a cleverly presented gnostic-type of play on the opposing definitions of public and private revelation (in Rome's Millennial Fatima Message) leads an ordinary person to conclude that somehow Lucia imagined or imaged some type of spiritual experience into her childish dreams and "visions." [This theory is reminiscent of Bultmann's (and the Novus Ordo) theory of scriptural formation.]

According to current ecclesial propaganda, the Fatima Message, in itself, is of doubtful meaning and significance. What is one to believe? *"We, the 'living magisterium;' we, the reigning liberal experts, will provide an 'interpretation of tongues.' We will clear all doubts and tell you what she said, meant to say and should have said."* [Welcome to Orwell's *1984!* Welcome to Pope/Rome's 1984!]

Has Rome's Millennial Fatima Message overstretched credibility? Even Marco Politi, co-author of a biography favorable to Pope John Paul II, declared that *"The vision of a pope being killed by solders with guns and arrows has nothing to do with the assassination attempt of 1981"* (*London Daily Telegraph,* June 27, 2000).

Why not? The Pope was the victim of a madman's rage, not of the anti-Catholics, with whom the Pope ecumenates, even to the extent of joining them in worship. Obviously, Pope John Paul was not killed. Obviously, not one bishop, priest, etc. "died in the same way, one after another."

The uppermost clergy have insulted Catholics by demanding that they believe the unbelievable. Furthermore, previous to 2000, the uppermost clergy destroyed, blasphemed and sacrileged Holy Mass and Holy Church. Now, Pope/Rome's Millennial Fatima Message adds Holy Mary to their list of blasphemed and sacrileged objects.

Having buried Holy Mass, Holy Mary and Holy Church, the establishment is now free to direct its efforts toward establishing and implementing the Novus Ordo Liturgy and Religion, along with the Novus Ordo political structure. This purpose can be perceived in the exegetical part of Rome's Millennial

Fatima Message. For example, in their interpretation of Rome's Third Secret, Cardinal Ratzinger and Archbishop Bertone insist that the Fatima-promised *"time of violence, destruction and persecution"* is past and to be forgotten. Therefore, the Fatima Message is to be consigned to the "forgotten past."

> The history of an entire century [the past century] can be seen in this image [of the Pope having led us to the top of the mountain by defeating Communism] once and forever.
>
> **Cardinal Ratzinger**

An era of peace will be given mankind.
Our Lady of Fatima

God gives peace only as His existential church acts in faith, as the priest's first Communion   prayer professes:

> Lord...Look on the faith of Thy church and, accordingly grant us peace....

The present Pope is our "Adam."When the Pope decides to act in faith (for spiritual reasons or according to God-given Fatima "geopolitical strategy") he will become the Marian Pope whose faith will bring Fatima's Blessings.

CHAPTER 19

THE MEGA-PICTURE ACCORDING TO MALACHI MARTIN

Malachi Martin was a Vatican insider. Because he read the Third Secret, his information and comments are employed to introduce the bigger picture. Malachi Martin died a year before Pope/Rome's Millennial Fatima Message was promulgated.

Up until 1981, he [Pope John Paul II] **believed he had a long range solution to world problems. Then he was shot...He thought he had** [experienced] **the Fatima Vision...After this, he knew his pontificate wouldn't last a long time. He had** [resolved to pursue] **a new geopolitical purpose in life. He also knew that the Soviet Union was finished and that Russia wasn't. He set out, therefore, to exert as much geopolitical influence as he could. But, you see, there was a major flaw in his armor. He had one guiding thing–Solidarity...The difficulty is this** [that] **this Solidarnasz is a purely secular movement, nothing religious but he had cut his teeth on that organization. That's how they** [once had] **defeated the Stalinists in Poland...When he started in geopolitics he still relied on secular**

organizations. He wasn't acting merely and simply through faith, using the arms of faith. He was doing geopolitics. It was the geopolitics of reason ["this worldly" geopolitics], not the geopolitics of faith. By 1989 or so, he had become immersed in this geopolitics of reason.

Pope John Paul II was a great friend of Gorbachev; and he had become very close to the Americans; and, he relied on the secular [this world] movements to bring about the spiritual end. And it didn't happen! He made a big mistake, the same mistake that Paul VI and John XXIII made...

The Queen of Heaven gave a mandate. She said 'Consecrate Russia to me one day, all bishops together, and Russia will be converted to Catholicism. It will become Catholic; and there will be no more chastisements. If you do not do so, God will punish you all...John XXIII said the children didn't know what Our Lady said. They thought Russia was a whore in the streets of Lisbon; and I'm talking to Nikita Kruschev. This was 1962, the time of the Vatican Council, and he [Kruschev] will allow [Orthodox] observers to come to my council if I don't condemn Russia. So he [Pope John XXIII] didn't allow the council to condemn Marxism; and, he would not publish the letter [the real Third Secret] ever. [He said to himself:] 'I will not consecrate Russia. If I did that, I know Nikita Kruschev would consider it an act of war...That's John XXIII for you...

Paul VI was afraid of his own shadow. He didn't believe in Fatima. John Paul II "sort of" believed in Fatima. He [felt he] couldn't do it [the Fatima Consecration of Russia] since he wasn't the pope of 1960...In fact, he permitted the suppression of Sr. Lucy and the suppression of the Fatima Message...His Secretary of State, Casaroli, who's an atheist, as far as I'm concerned, also suppressed Fatima...all he could do in St. Peter's Square [in 1984] in the middle of a consecration of the world is say 'We also entrust to your care those people who are awaiting our consecration [of them] to the Immaculate Heart...To me, this is gobblygook and disgusts me [Malachi Martin]...I think it all goes back to Lucifer. He just has too much power within the prelacy of the church.

He has paralyzed and frustrated what the Mother of God wants...They [these three popes] had no trust in God. It's clear to me these three popes set about [determined] to destroy the organization of the Church of Christ, which they have done...They're not supposed to do that...He [John Paul II] rejected spiritual means given by Our Lady. He didn't do what she said: to consecrate Russia with all of his bishops on the same day...[one reason] Vatican powers are totally penetrated with Masonry....

Malachi Martin, *The Temptor's Hour* (Tape 2) available from Catholic Treasures, 1-800-257-4893

Apocalypse Now
Satan Versus Holy Mass and Holy Mary

What Satan began by the Protestant Revolt, he is now bringing to perfection through the Bishops' Novus Ordo Liturgical Revolt. Luther vowed to destroy Holy Church by destroying Holy Mass: " *Tolle missam, tolle ecclesiam!*" Now Luther's desire, (also Satan's desire) has been fulfilled. Holy Mass has been removed from the establishment church. In its place are a cacophony or legion of Novus Ordo mass-like liturgies. As with the Protestant Revolt, so with the Bishops' Revolt: as Holy Mass is destroyed, proper and full devotion to Holy Mary is destroyed.

However, Our Lady of Fatima has assured us that when enough are sufficiently praying and sacrificing, the Marian Popes will appear. These Popes, being devoted to Holy Mass and Holy Mary, will embrace the Fatima Opportunity of rePARation. Consequently, they will bring back (bring up to par) Holy Church and thereby, Holy Mass, Holy Mary, Holy Russia.

Imagine salvation history from God's view. After centuries of preparation, through God's boundless love, His Saving Will, His Saving Event, His Saving Person was incarnated on earth as in eternal heaven. Then came the Bishops' Revolt (in the 1960's). Now, Daniel's prophecy as professed by all of the Church Fathers is materializing. Now, Satan has thwarted God's Salutary Will. Now, Genesis is being fulfilled. A decisive battle is being waged between Satan and Our Lady of the Canonized Mass. Now is the Apocalypse, as Sister Lucy said to Father Fuentes in 1957: (cf. Apoc 12; 13)

> **Father, the devil is currently engaged in a decisive battle with the Virgin.**
> **Sister Lucy, 1957**

In order to understand salvation history and even the Fatima Message, one must understand Genesis: the first and well-known prophecy and curse of God. St. Louis-Marie wrote of this:

> **We should understand the first and well-known prophecy and curse of God: the perpetual enmity that He put between Satan and the Mother of God. This is the root of the enmity between the children of Satan and the children of Mary–that is, between the friends of this world and all Christians.**
>
> **He outlined the kind of devotion and service of Jesus through Mary that all faithful Christians ought to embrace, to prepare themselves for this battle; then, he wrote: 'Then they will clearly see that beautiful Star of the Sea, as much as faith allows...They will experience her**

motherly kindness and affection for her children. They will love her tenderly and will appreciate how full of compassion she is and how much they stand in need of her help.'

And there's another prophecy in the manuscript, one that has its echoes in all of the saint's written works about the coming Marian age. 'Mary must be known and openly revealed by the Holy Spirit so that Jesus may be known, loved and served through her. This will happen, especially, toward the end of the world.'

Holy Virginity, St. Louis-Marie de Montfort

Under and through Our Lady of the Canonized Mass, Mary's Remnant wages the ultimate battle. Now and increasingly in the future, many Catholics, deprived of Holy Mass, can fight effectively only with the Rosary. God has shown the power of the Rosary prayed with devotion to the Immaculata. At Hiroshima and Nagasaki, praying the Rosary physically saved Mary's Remnant. How much more will praying the Rosary save those who will no longer be able to pray Holy Mass?

There will come a time when all you will have is the Rosary and devotion to My Immaculate Heart.

Our Lady of Fatima

These times are now. The apocalypse is now.

CHAPTER 20

CONVERSION AS ENVISAGED BY THE FATIMA CONSECRATION

**In the end, my Immaculate Heart will triumph.
Russia will be converted and an era of peace
will be granted to mankind.**
Our Lady of Fatima

The Fatima-predicted apocalyptic scenario is: the proper Fatima-commanded consecration of Russia to the Immaculate Heart of Mary; Russia's subsequent conversion; and the birth of "Holy Russia." Then, a restored Holy Church and a "repared" Latin or Holy Eastern Church will convert most or all of the world, so that a period of peace will ensue.

What is most likely the major liturgy of conversion according to God's choice? How must it be used to convert Russia and the world? Are leaders of the Eastern Liturgy (the Orthodox) wicked heretics: non-

Catholic or even anti-Catholic (similar to Novus Ordo Church leaders?

The Fatime Apocalypse Liturgy of God's Choice

It is not likely that Russia will convert to the Canonized Latin Mass Liturgy. Rather, Russia will be graced into embracing, in freedom, purity and peace, the Canonized Eastern Rite Liturgy and Religion, basically that of St. John Chrysostom and St. Basil.

Most likely, in the era of Fatima Blessings, the Canonized Eastern Rite Liturgy will be employed by Russia's clergy, religious and dedicated laity to convert much of the world to Catholicism. (Such a conversion is necessary so that the last part of Our Lady's Third Secret text may be fulfilled: namely, that the world will enjoy a period of peace.)

Unlike the liturgically heretical Novus Ordo west, the east does not need liturgical reparation. There is no indication that the east has not retained the Canonized Mass Liturgy (in its eastern modality or expression) intact: in its pristine "Apostolic expression" or canonized form (words). Before the takeover of Russia's Errors,

Russian Orthodoxy always was in agreement with and acceptable to the Holy See.

> **The Russian Orthodox Church separated from the Holy See only *de facto* (there was no direct formal breach between the Sees of Rome and Moscow) so that, one can profess the totality of Catholic doctrine and be in communion with the Holy See while continuing to be Russian Orthodox.**
> See Soloviev, Website: http://rumkatkilise.org/raya byzantium.htm

Lex orandi, lex credendi: as one prays the liturgy, so does one believe. The intact Canonized Eastern Liturgy has impregnated and fed salutary faith and morals into the souls of its priests and laymen.

Eastern churches need to exist in social peace and autonomous freedom–freedom from state and "other rite" hostile forces. In Fatima's terms, the Eastern Liturgy needs to be freed from Russia's Errors: the various types of subjection to evil ecclesial gnostic powers (neo-scholastic and neo-Hegelian wicked churchmen, especially, those who, in effect, emanate from the "anti-Christ see or seat of Rome," to use La Salette's terms); and, from the various agnostic and dictatorial governmental rules of modern "enlightened man" (as incarnated in such infamous "humanity loving but God rejecting" dictators as Hitler, Stalin and Gorbachev).

Will the Eastern Canonized Liturgy (Holy Mass) freed from Russia's Errors become the liturgy of Russia's conversion? Will the Canonized Latin Mass Liturgy (Holy Mass)–(the Latin Patriarchate freed from the Novus Ordo tragedy) become the liturgy of Russia's conversion?

The essential Fatima challenge is for the Pope to operate "religiously or from faith, " not from political expediency. The Pope must be "prayed and sacrificed" out of the pursuit of natural geopolitics and into embracing the supernatural God-given Fatima opportunity/command. The Pope who does this will be the Marian Pope.

In effect, Pope/Rome has officially committed itself to the use of the Canonized Eastern Mass Liturgy in Russia. The official church policy regarding the Eastern Liturgy, laws and established customs is that the Eastern Liturgy should remain intact. All that is required is a more formalized union with Rome. This was expressed by Pope St. Pius X in his dictum regarding the "conversion" or more formalized union of eastern church (es) with Pope/Rome. The eastern churches are to retain their liturgy, laws and established customs *"nec plus, nec minus, nec aliter. "*

Western Catholics need to renounce the evil spirit of

Vatican Two by embracing the eastern "prayer-set." Because of evil-spirited gnosticism in the form of neo-scholasticism and neo-Hegelianism, the Latin Rite Patriarchate has, in effect (or in practice), denounced and rejected its Christ-given patrimony: the Christ-given Canonized Latin Mass Liturgy.

On the other hand, the east has retained its conviction that Divine Liturgy is the work (ergos) of praising God (laos), not as in the New Order travesty, where liturgy is defined as the work of the people. In the east, God is central. God is the Sustainer, Inspirer, Summit and very *"raison d'etre"* of eastern religion: of eastern spiritual life; of eastern asceticism; and of the eastern expression of the Divine Liturgy. The eastern prayer-set expresses man's sinfulness and insufficiency before Christ, man's only Saviour.

> **The Fathers of the East start with the awareness that authentic spiritual commitment can not be reduced to an encounter with oneself, to an even necessary recovery of interiority, but must be a journey of docile listening to the Spirit of God. In fact, they maintain, man is not completely himself if he is closed to the Holy Spirit. St. Irenaeus, Bishop of Lyons, who, because of his origins and formation, can be considered a bridge between East and West, saw man as made up of three elements: body, soul and Holy Spirit (cf.** *Adversus*

haereses 5,9,1,-20). Certainly, he did not intend to confuse man with God, but he was concerned to emphasize that man reaches his fullness only by opening himself to God. For Aphraates of Persia, who echoes St. Paul's thought, the Spirit of God is offered to us in such an intimate way as to become almost part of our 'self' (cf. *Demonstrationes* 6,14). In the same sense, a Russian spiritual author, Theophane the Recluse, reached the point of calling the Holy Spirit 'the soul of the human soul' and saw the purpose of the spiritual life in a 'gradual spiritualization of the soul and of the body' (cf. *Letters on Spiritual Life*). The true enemy of the interior ascent is sin. It must be overcome in order to make room for the Spirit of God.

Pope John Paul II, Angelus address, Sept. 8, 1996

Regarding the Pope's last observation, note that "sin, man's only enemy and the only evil" can be overcome, defeated or removed, only by or through, the Holy Sacrifice. In our "Apocalypse now," Our Lady of the Canonized Mass comes to remove "tables and happy meals" from her Son's churches and to restore altars upon which validly ordained priests will offer the Holy Sacrifice for the forgiveness of sins by saying the Canonized Latin or Eastern Mass Liturgy.

Indeed, sin is the only apocalyptic evil. In Tillich's words, each man is naturally estranged from God, from the ground of his being. Man is a sinner by birth, and by inclination; as well as, in deed and in habit. Each Sunday is designed by God for man that he may, mystically and by anticipation, confront the Blessed Kingdom through the Divine Liturgy of the Holy Sacrifice, effective unto the removal of his sins; his sinfulness and the eternal effect of sin.

> **The sense of liturgy is particularly vivid among our Eastern brothers and sisters. For them, the liturgy is truly 'heaven on earth'** *(Orientale lumen, n. 11).* **It is a synthesis of the whole faith experience. It is an involving experience which touches the whole human person, body and soul. Everything in the sacred action aims at expressing 'the divine harmony and the model of humanity transfigured:' 'the shape of the church, the sounds, the colors, the lights, the scents. The lengthy duration of the celebration itself and the repeated invocations express the progressive identification with the mystery celebrated with one's whole person'** (cf. ibid).
> **Pope John Paul II, Angelus address, Nov. 3, 1996**

Eastern Divine Liturgy is a matter of the heart. In God-given, Apostolic-formed Divine Liturgy, one's heart is mystically united with the Sacred Heart and the Immaculate Heart. Eastern Liturgy is Apostolic in origin. It comes to us a "finished product, great and tender, with the charm of sublimity and the beauty of asceticism, with a seriousness that is never ponderous and a refinement that is never labored–and all touched for our vision with the beauty of 'blue distance'" (*Byzantine Church and Culture*, Archbishop Raya, Alleluia Press, 1992).

Holy Mary's Fatima Apocalypse

In the west, the ongoing urgent salutary need is to attain and deepen within each Catholic, the Canonized Mass "prayer-set," which will destroy the prevalent "gnostic mind-set," which decimated the Latin Rite Patriarchate. Even under Communism, Eastern Uniate and Orthodox Catholics have survived and prospered (in the midst of Russia's Errors) because of their "Holy Mary Holy Mass Liturgical Prayer-set." The current lack of religious prosperity in the Church will be provided through the rise of Marian Popes.

Of course, in the era of Fatima Blessings, the Canonized Latin Mass Rite will be restored to its proper exclusive place in the Latin Rite. The Novus Ordo tragedy will be anathematized. The existential church will be the one and only Church, outside of which there exists no salvation.

Nec Plus   Nec Minus   Nec Aliter

Should a properly functioning Pope/Rome accept and welcome an "eastern liturgical conversion" of Russia and many others? The liturgies of Trent and St. John Chrysostom (the typical form of Eastern Liturgy) are equally canonized Catholic liturgies. Each has its proper role, nature and effectiveness. The great saint and popular Slavophile, Pope St. Pius X, expressed the mind and heart of Our Lady of the Canonized Mass (east and west) in this matter:

> **On May 22, 1908, Fr. Zerchaniniv was appointed the Administrator of the Mission to the Russian Catholics. The decree from the Vatican Secretariat of State appointing him specifically states: 'Therefore, His Holiness commands the aforementioned priest Zerchaninov to observe the laws of the Greek-Slavonic Rite faithfully and in all their integrity, without any admixture from the Latin Rite or any other Rite; he must also see that his subjects, clergy and all other Catholics do the same.'**
> http://rumkatkilise.org/rayabyzantium.htm

Subsequently, this command to observe strictly the Russian Orthodox Church's ecclesial government, rituals and spirituality was confirmed during an audience with

Pope Pius X attended by Mlle. Ushakova. Mll. Ushakova's inquired as to whether the Russian Catholics should hold firmly to their Russian synodal and Old Ritualist practices, or adapt these to the more "latinized" liturgical forms.

Pope Pius X replied that the Russian Catholics should adhere to the synodal and Old Rite practices. In his now famous response in Latin, Pope (St.) Pius X stated: *"...nec plus, nec minus, nec aliter" (no more, no less, no different)*. This essential Catholic principle will be observed and enforced by the glorious Marian Pope.

Nec plus, nec minus; nec aliter. Every Catholic must accept the pure, integral and Apostolic Eastern Liturgies as "irreplaceably canonical." They are not defective and need not be replaced by the Canonized Latin Mass Liturgy. The "profound simplicity" of the Canonized Eastern Liturgy complements and does not threaten the "inexhaustibly deep" Canonized Latin Mass Liturgy.

Formally Schismatic   Not Heretical

A major problem arises in the minds of some older Catholics or brainwashed western Catholics: *"How can fiducial union exist? Were we not taught that Russians rejected the 'Immaculata' and 'filioque?' Are they not heretics?"* To treat this objection in any detail would be too far afield of the Fatima topic.

Realize that even as one might have been taught that eastern orthodoxy held heresies, one was also assured that they were merely schismatic (at least, formally). These Catholic mentors were inconsistent.

Note, also, that the Eastern Canonized Liturgy, which is far more devoted to Holy Mary than the western Canonized Latin Liturgy, can hardly be accused of heresy, especially, when the Liturgy often fervently and liturgically prays to the "ever Virgin and ever sinless" Mary, Mother of God. Similar remarks can be made about the "filioque issue." Again, any final resolution of doctrinal conflict will determine that eastern belief complements rather than denies the true faith.

> **In a joint declaration, Pope John Paul and Catholicos Karekin II have acknowledged each other's religious traditions, saying that their doctrines are 'complementary rather than in opposition.' The Pope and the Armenian Church leader 'together confess' their faith in God, in Jesus Christ, and in 'one, holy, catholic, and apostolic Church.' They explicitly recognize the validity of each other's**

sacraments, and promise to intensify their search for closer communion, noting that each Church has a great deal to offer the other.
Catholic World Report, Dec. 2000

Moreover, since *lex orandi, lex credendi* holds true, any religious disunity with Rome has been mainly political or "only *de facto.*" Disunity (not subjected to Russia's Errors) has never been spiritual nor seriously or essentially religious.

Also, it would seem, Our Lady of the (Eastern) Canonized Mass is completing what God began immediately before the Communist takeover. Our Lady's Fatima Blessing will bestow formal reunion of orthodox communities (freed from the oppression of Russia's Error) and Rome; and a purified or "restored" Latin Rite Patriarchate.

This chapter ends as it began–looking forward to the fulfilment of the Third Secret's final sentence, Holy Mary's Fatima Apocalypse:

> **In the end, my Immaculate Heart will triumph. Russia will be converted and an era of peace will be granted to mankind.**
> **Our Lady of Fatima**

SPECIAL OFFER!

ALL 3: BOOK + VIDEO + AUDIO= $33
Postage included.

FR. PAUL TRINCHARD BOOKS & TAPES:

See MAETA color catalog on the internet:

WWW.MAETA.COM

See order form on web site

E-MAIL YOUR ORDER TO:

maeta@flash.net

or FAX IT:
1-504-833-5272

TOLL FREE CREDIT CARD ORDERS ONLY:

1-888-577-4428

MAETA is a 501 (3) (c) non-profit.
Donations are tax deductible according to the rules of the IRS.

Make your tax deductible contribution to MAETA.
Buy MAETA books & tapes for yourself & others.

M A r i a n   E n d   T i m e s   A p o s t o l a t e

LIGHT A CANDLE!

BUY MAETA BOOKS & PAMPHLETS!

FOR YOURSELF & OTHERS

Spread the word!

TOLL FREE–CREDIT CARD ORDERS ONLY:
1-888-577-4428
Use Mailing Label Below for Mail Orders

MAETA PO BOX   6012   METAIRIE LA 70009-6012

----

name_____

address_____

city_____state_____zip_____-_____